FRANK FIELD has been Member of Parliament for Birkenhead since 1979. He Chaired the Health and Social Security Select Committee before becoming Minister for Welfare Reform in Tony Blair's first Government.

His previous books, like this one, aimed at understanding emerging issues, changing attitudes and helping shape Government policy.

Neighbours from Hell:

The politics of behaviour

Frank Field MP

POLITICO'S

First published in Great Britain 2003 by
Politico's Publishing, an imprint of
Methuen Publishing Limited
215 Vauxhall Bridge Road
London SW1V 1EJ

10 9 8 7 6 5 4 3 2 1

A CIP catalogue record for this book is available from the British Library

ISBN 1 84275 078 X

Printed and bound in Great Britain by Cox and Wyman

Contents

Preface

A number of people have helped me to produce *Neighbours from Hell*. Jill Hendey has borne the major task of typing the various drafts and, with Adam Gray, was responsible for the final preparation of the manuscript for the printers. Adam kindly read through the entire draft and improved the presentation of the argument as did Ben Forsyth. Damian Leeson read part of the book when it was in draft and he improved its clarity. Sally Broadbent and other researchers in the House of Commons Library found information for me. While I am extremely grateful to all of these individuals, the citations are not intended to reflect away from myself the final responsibility for how the arguments are set out on the following pages.

Frank Field
July 2003

1. The new politics of behaviour

Introduction

The old politics of class, it was claimed, was swept away by the Third Way. But today's political agenda is no longer just about finding a compromise between socialism and capitalism. Increasingly the new politics is about moderating behaviour and re-establishing the social virtues of self-discipline coupled with an awareness of the needs of others. It is these virtues above all others which are essential to civilised living. The new politics centre on reinforcing what is good and acceptable behaviour.

The forward march halted

Edmund Burke observed that the most dangerous of all revolutions was that in the sentiments, manners and moral opinion of the citizenry. The first signs of such a revolution are now apparent in Britain. A degree of respect and civility in the behaviour of one person to another is crucial to the wellbeing of us all. That respect was not established easily or quickly. Britain began its long march to respectable behaviour over two hundred years ago.

This long march to respectability is a grand tale recording, amongst other events, an ever-increasing number of families teaching their children a set of values which I call here social virtues or common decencies. These virtues, which became almost universally practiced, ensured that the family's behaviour promoted a thoughtfulness for its other members as well as its neighbours. But the attitudes, behaviour and customs thus established are under threat.

A growing number of families no longer understand the importance of these virtues to their neighbour's immediate wellbeing, or to their own family's interests. In a significant respect, the drive to respectability has not only been thwarted but has gone into reverse. *Neighbours from Hell* records not only happens when these virtues are no longer practiced, but also sets out the role government might play in first countering and then reversing this cycle of decline.

A key aspect in the long march to what Britons saw as respectability has been a growth of respect for others, the origins of which lie deep in the development of respect for oneself. That growth in dual responsibility, to oneself and to others, has involved a voluntary acceptance of restrictions on what each of us as individuals should and should not do. Central to the counter-revolution against common decency is the collapse of a proper consideration of others. Life lived in the absence of such self-imposed rules of behaviour is becoming for a persistent, but increasing minority, a normal state of existence. Invariably bound up, and reinforcing this trend, has been a loss of people's ability to think over the long-term as a factor in judging one's own behaviour. Living for the moment blocks any recognition of the severe downside to the loss of social virtues.

We have as a country so taken for granted the exercise of those virtues that writing about their failure to be transmitted successfully from one generation to another is difficult. To begin a proper discussion on this requires the redevelopment of a language long since fallen into disuse. These social virtues or personal values were so successfully transmitted from parents to children that there was little to be discussed, and there was consequently no call for a public debate. Society worked well in this most crucial respect. End of conversation.

Within a decade the scene has begun to deteriorate, bringing with it more than a menacing threat for the immediate future and beyond. There is no one specific event that accounts for the swiftness of this turn around. A number of social landmines lay buried in our culture awaiting the moment to explode. These explosions have come in quick succession.

That all values are internal to ourselves, and that there are no absolute truths to draw upon, has long been part of a public debate in Britain. Emmanuel Kant brought the Enlightenment to its head by insisting on the moral autonomy of man. We shall see later how this once small tributary of an idea has reached the broad mouth of the river where the rushing water sings to the tune of 'my views are just as good as yours'.

It was only a matter of time before Christian belief felt the effects of the Kantian revolution. Yet when, for a growing group of the population in this country, faith became doubt, the hope of the most thoughtful doubters was that most of Christian morality would survive without the underpinning of Christian dogma and belief. The wonder is not that what is loosely thought of as Christian morality is in such a rapid and widespread retreat in parts of

Britain. The surprise is that it served so long as a force for good after the perishing of its spiritual and intellectual roots.

As the roar of faith's receding tide echoed around society's institutions, much of the worship of God beyond the skies became rooted in radical politics. Working people designed a better world for themselves and their comrades by building a mutual commonwealth. Within this ethical furnace the building bricks of national duties were forged. The 1945 Attlee government not only nationalised the basic industries but, more importantly, nationalised this moral commonwealth, replacing localised responsibilities with a remote, state controlled system of welfare. The impact on personal behaviour of stripping out from society mutually owned organisation now becomes ever more apparent.

The change in social attitudes from the 1960s has had so many beneficial effects in respect of personal freedom and often happiness. But these changes have not come without cost, although the size of the price ticket is only now becoming apparent. The convention which in one instance curtailed an individual's freedom of action, and came under attack for that very reason, protected many more individuals from unwanted and uninvited attention.

Investment in children during their first years of life has also changed. The pressure for mothers (or fathers) to return to work quickly can have costs for children. The intense efforts which carers put into forming the best pattern of behaviour in children is easily lost if both parents work early in a child's life. Because it has been assumed that good parenting is acquired by osmosis, benchmarks on best practice are not systematically taught as they should be, as part of the national curriculum or included in ante- or post-natal classes.

The impact of Thatcherism is also part of our present discontent. State collectivism had more than run its course by the early 1970s, but Labour was blind to the need to show that its core collective provision beliefs could still enhance freedom. The ration book approach to public services was hung onto like a political comfort blanket. The remnants of ration book socialism, except for the National Health Service, were swept away by the Thatcher revolution. In an almost allergic reaction to the collectivism of Mr Attlee, Thatcherism became the engine force behind the idea that collectivism was the antithesis of individual freedoms.

A new balance between freedom and regulation was proper and overdue, but the new cult of individualism was fostered as though the whole of our lives can be lived in seconds, unrelated to the days of our being. It is these days which demand a collective sense of our existence. Without these collective checks individual freedom begins its descent into anarchy. That anarchy is the sworn enemy of social virtues.

Transmitting virtue

Manners, sentiments and moral opinions are learned best in families. It is the breakdown in a growing number of families in the teaching of social virtues which is becoming a central issue to voters. To talk of transmitting social virtues is already a foreign language to a minority, but growing number of households. Once the great chain of social progress, linking one generation's wisdom to the next, is broken, families cease to function in their vital role as transmitters of social virtues. A new norm of 'acceptable' behaviour is quickly established in which the cultivation of those social virtues, centring around a respect for others, plays increasingly less of a role, or no role at all.

A central question for the early decades of the twenty first century in Britain, and I imagine in many other countries as well, is what role can politics have where families have failed? Much of post-war political activity has been seen in terms of high politics, or in macro terms, and this is as true for domestic as it has been for foreign policy. Considering politics in this fashion is crucially important, but it does not constitute by any stretch of the imagination the total sum of what politics is.

The most important change in economic policy during the past thirty years has been a move towards micro economic considerations. The instigators of the Institute of Economic Affairs, reflecting on their success, have written that the macro economy is in fact made up of a host of micro decisions made by individuals and that, by inference, economic policy should be about helping those individuals achieve success. A similar change in thinking wrought by the IEA to the economy is urgently required in respect to our social thinking. To refashion a well known phrase, there is no society without individuals, families and neighbourhoods. *Neighbours from Hell* is an exercise in micro politics and is concerned exclusively with devising policies so that the decent majority can repel the advance of the scarcely disguised semi-barbarian forces.

This micro politics is about laying the basis for a more widespread transference of the key social virtues. Some commentators see society in terms of a river. But rivers without banks are a contradiction in terms; they quickly become a flood with all the disastrous consequences which follow from that. Over time all rivers wear away their banks, and if they are to remain rivers those banks need watching and repairing. So too with society. Society's banks are made up of conventions, customs and laws. If it is not to disintegrate into greater lawlessness and a form of slow burning anarchy, society's banks need watching and repairing. It is about such work that this book is concerned.

The Plan

This demise of a universally practised consideration for other people – for that is what is happening – is greeted by the majority of us with more despair than fury. Fury there often is at the way normal decent life is being ferreted away. But despair is the more prevalent reaction. Who understands? Who intends to act against this growing barbarism which appears ready to sweep all before it in our country?

This tract is the record of one MP as he has observed events and tried to reconstruct a language which could convey something of the degree to which the established order of his constituents' lives has been broken asunder. I was at first shocked by the behaviour which perceptively began taking on a new and grotesque face during the 1992 Parliament. Shock turned to anger at the unfairness of what I was called upon to observe by constituents. There was anger too at the impotence I felt when authority, which included myself, was found to be without adequate weapons with which to fight back. There could be no fight back without changes to current policies and practices. *Neighbours from Hell* tries to sketch out a map of this new country as well as the decisive steps in the route march back to the decent world we are fast leaving behind.

The debate opens by looking into the abyss and relaying what life is like for those who are continually on the sharp end of anti-social behaviour. This is not a detailed audit of what is happening. The aim is to provide a survey of the main contours of a fast changing social landscape. *Neighbours from Hell* then considers the virtues once so widely practised, which made up the backbone of common decencies in this country.

The book then reflects on what makes anti-social behaviour different from actions which have been traditionally punished through the legal system, before weighing up the arguments which are already emerging on why governments should not be concerned with the kind of people its citizenry should be. *Neighbours from Hell* then marshals the evidence to show that, far from the new politics being an attack on the poor, it is the poor who will most benefit and who demand most fervently the advent of an effective counter-strategy to anti-social behaviour.

At the heart of *Neighbours from Hell* is an argument that politics has to once again make central to its actions an assessment of what kind of people we need to be to inhabit a peaceable kingdom. How to initiate a national debate on this new kind of politics becomes the first consideration. *Neighbours from Hell*'s central thesis is a consideration of what can replace the largely beneficial effect evangelical Christianity and mutually owned welfare once played in moulding civilised behaviour in Britain. In doing so the book proposes that, where parents have failed, the police should take on the role of surrogate parents. It proposes a new step change in the contractual basis on which welfare is received so that it gains a major role again in teaching what does and does not constitute acceptable behaviour. Lastly, *Neighbours from Hell* suggests a number of ways in which education can play the role of parent, where parents fail to carry out the most necessary of tasks in nurturing their young.

2. The rise and rise of anti-social behaviour

Introduction

What my constituents see as politics has changed out of all recognition during the 20 years or so since I first became their Member of Parliament. From a traditional fare of social security complaints, housing transfers, unfair dismissals, as well as job loses, constituents now, more often than not, ask what can be done to stop their lives being made a misery by the unacceptable behaviour of some neighbours, or more commonly, their neighbours' children. The aim here is not to present a detailed survey. The purpose is to provide an overall view of how the collapse of decent behaviour impacts on the lives of decent citizens.

Politics changes

The moment I realised society was unquestionably changing for the worse is still indelibly etched on my memory. I hold my surgeries at

Birkenhead town hall and into the small office I occupy came a group of pensioners well into their 70s. I can see their movements now as though it was yesterday. The politeness as the women came to the door first. Those with the most marked disability were effortlessly guided to the available chairs which faced the desk I borrow for the session. Each of the pensioners were immaculately dressed in their best clothes to see their MP. The contrast between these most respectable working class gentlemen and women and the behaviour of the young fiends whose activities they went on to describe could not have been more marked – despite their living side by side.

There has always been some disorder in the town. Weekends are particularly bad, and never more so than when the pubs and clubs reach the throwing out hour. The list of the big 'do nots' can be read from the charge sheet at the local bridewell, which now masquerades under the boastful title of the custody suite. Rarely, thank goodness, is anyone arrested for murder. But the entry of theft on the inmates' board is all too common.

Almost all the custody suite's temporary residents are there because of drink, or drugs, even though this root cause of their arrest makes only a fleeting appearance on the blackboards which record the cell into which they have been placed. Here then is one glimpse of what is now regarded as the traditional pattern of crime, against which the forces of law and order have built up defences for almost as long as mankind has lived together in groups on these islands.

The circumstances described by this small group of pensioners catapulted me into a different world and laid the foundations for *Neighbours from Hell*. Nothing had prepared me for the description of what they were enduring and the hell which had engulfed them. Young lads who ran across their bungalow roofs, peed through their letterboxes, jumped out of the shadows as they returned home at night, and, when they were watching television, tried to break their sitting room windows, presumably with the hope of showering the pensioners with shattered glass.

Their faces bore witness to this tragedy. They had expected to live out their time in peace and dignity. Their basic sense of justice was affronted. They had worked hard all their lives, always adding more to society than they ever took from it. They had behaved respectfully to their elders. They reasonably expected to be similarly treated. The lady nearest me nervously plucked at her handbag straps. Each face was lined with strain. Most of their eyes were red from being robbed of the certainty of sleep.

The police, they reported, could do nothing. The young people knew their rights. They could not be touched. The visit of these constituents resulted in what has so far been an eight year campaign to try and persuade governments that politics has entered a new and darker age.

Politics changes gear

The issues which my constituents now raise with me have changed beyond all recognition over the 23 years I have represented them in parliament. During my first decade as MP the work was tough only because of the sheer weight of the numbers of enquiries. Housing, social security and employment were all issues which constituents raised.

No matter how complicated the issue I could always provide an answer, even if my constituents didn't always like how I responded. My best answers came from Nick Warren, the most talented welfare rights lawyer in the country, with whom I worked for well over half of my parliamentary life. Slowly at first, then in a great tide like the one which confronted Noah, the issue of disorder began to swamp the agenda.

I no longer had answers to give to my constituents. Without rethinking what politics should be about I could extend no hope to meet their quite proper demands for a civilised existence. Robberies, fights and a few murders, as the custody suite's list of inmates testifies, are still part of the scene. Over centuries our legal system has evolved to deal with this kind of traditional disorder. But bad behaviour, which makes normal life impossible for those caught on the receiving end, has not until recently been so prevalent that citizens require protection. Now the innocent are being systematically targeted.

It is here that the new politics are being forged. Discovering a Third Way proved a good rallying cry to shoehorn out the Tory government which had over-stayed its welcome, but it provides no map or compass to this unknown political terrain which voters are currently left largely to negotiate on their own. Some of the older established issues continue. But generally the new politics centres on behaviour, or rather, its collapse.

Harassment after school

There had been recent discussion as to how children should be punished for abusing and assaulting teachers. I think that children should be named and shamed in the same way teachers are if they abuse/assault children, or even if they are simply accused of doing so!

I am a teacher at a local secondary school (in Crewe) and live near the school. There are also some of the children I teach who live nearby.

There is a gang of 15/16 year old children who I teach who have for some months now constantly and relentlessly harassed me! When I take my dog for a walk they will follow me for a while, shouting comments and throw small things at me such as chewing gum, tightly rolled up bits of paper etc. When I go to the shops with my young daughter or with family members, the same things happen.

My parents also receive abuse when out with their dogs. Only the other day they were out and a member of this gang shouted out to them, 'Oi you, we hate your fucking daughter'. There was nothing they could do about this!

I have contacted the police who tell me there is nothing they can do! I have spoken to a solicitor who also says there is nothing I can do. I have even contacted my teaching union who are also helpless! So, it would seem that I must continue to put up with this bullying, abuse and assault and these youngsters will never have to face the consequences of their anti-social and indeed criminal acts!!

If a child lied through its teeth and simply accused me of any of these acts, I bet within the hour I'd be in a police cell, jobless and considered a threat to society and to my community etc. As of yet I have not retaliated and have remained professional at all times! But crimes continue to be committed against me and it would appear I have no rights, but children have many!

Teachers are now being given the joy (?) of teaching citizenship in school. How the hell do I teach citizenship to youngsters who are allowed to go out of the school gate and do as they please? They are fully aware of the fact that they can get away with almost anything, and never have to face the consequences of their acts!

Those who arty-farty round children's rights, etc, need to take a long hard look at what is going on. We will regret this, we are bringing up a generation who really believe that they can do as they please, and indeed they can and do!

My current situation is causing me dilemmas! Do I leave my job? Why should I? I love my job and the majority of pupils at my school are well behaved young people! Moving home isn't an option either. But surely I can't be expected to continue to put up with this forever more or for as long as I live and teach here?

A teacher from Crewe

Yobbism's unacceptable face

The face of the new politics belongs to Jason. He was my first introduction to a destroyer of peace and order for whom no laws then existed to control his behaviour.

Jason, then all of thirteen years of age, had been busy with his mates, pelting local residents with slates as they tried to go about their business and to the local store. Standing on the roof of a nearby deserted pub, Jason and his not so merry band of accomplices, pelted local shoppers. They won. The business closed and only then did the gang descend from their temporary home. Under what was then the existing law, the police were unable to do anything effective, and Jason realised this early on.

I first learned that the business was about to go under from a phone call from the owner. Her hard work in building up a viable general store, in an area which made that far from certain, was about to collapse. On the heels of that phone call the local residents came to see me at one of my surgeries at the town hall. It was a large group of upright citizens, some younger than me (that becomes ever more common now), some older.

The younger ones, I judged, could well look after themselves. But, as they explained, they took great care in coming to see me. To have acted otherwise would have attracted the gang's attention and a series of counter-offensives would have quickly followed. I was assured that, for the same reason, the same carefulness not to draw attention to themselves would be followed on the return journey.

The words tumbled out in a mixture of raw anger and despair. 'Who would have thought that this is how we would end up?' was a common refrain. It is just in the last few years, I was emphatically told, that it all went haywire. 'People talk of things collapsing like a house of cards. They are dead right, except it is my life that has gone, not simply cards.'

Jason, if not already, will very shortly be an alcoholic. Like all too many very young teenagers across the country alcohol gives him a quick buzz, and a buzz is the key determinant of what is and what is not done. Cheap double strength cider is sold in an increasing array of stores and off licences. One litre of this deadly mixture goes for a pound. Licensing committees have very little power to limit the number of licences. A refusal is quickly appealed and appeals are almost always successful.

Drinking amongst the gang is not a social experience. Unlike older people who learned to drink first with their parents and grandparents, and only then alone with their mates, drinking for Jason and his like is all about getting drunk as quickly as possible. As Jason is feared locally he can buy his alcohol as and when the fancy takes him, although he is clearly under-age.

Attack on public workers

Ray has worked as a paramedic at Birkenhead ambulance station for the best part of twenty years, which almost exactly parallels my time as the town's MP. He reports on the build-up of anti-social behaviour during that time, culminating in the town's ambulance station being temporarily closed. What is extraordinary is that this closure was as a result of continual wild aggression by children as young as eight or nine years.

What happened to the ambulance station in Birkenhead is not an isolated case in the town or, more importantly, in the country. A noticeable change in behaviour occurred well over a decade ago and was then simply dubbed as 'bad behaviour'. The ambulance workers' cars parked around the station became the target of attack. Twelve years ago the attacks became so sustained that the cars were moved into the station.

Then the station came under attack and defensive grills were screwed onto each of the windows, which proved an example of one step forward, two steps back. These security fences provided a means for access to the roof. Cars leaving the station were stoned. One ambulance worker was 'bricked' while working inside the station, and the new fuel tank came under bombardment. This slide into anarchy at the ambulance station is a parable for our time.

Given the worry of drunks dying by inhaling their own vomit, the police are naturally keen that the worst drunks should be taken to A&E or, possibly, home. If a drunk can fight there is little chance of them dying from their own vomit. Even so, the local police are more anxious to see younger drunks taken home by ambulance, according to paramedics, than into our new friend the custody suite. Angela, another paramedic, explained how when taking young drunks home it was not unknown, although thankfully uncommon, for a parent or grandparent to join in arguing with the ambulance staff, and sometimes fighting alongside the young drunk who becomes aggressive once again when back on home territory.

In Wirral alone there are already five households which ambulance crews will not attend without police protection. It is not a question of the crews attending unannounced or unsummoned. These are five families who are requesting the help of the ambulance service yet, despite such a request, behave in such a way, and have such a record of fighting and brawling with people who they see as carrying with them an authority, that the police have to be present to protect the ambulance staff as they take a member of the family to hospital. The mob rules even in cases of an extreme emergency and, even though a family member needs emergency treatment, attacks on staff from the families are more than a possibility.

These five families are, admittedly, extreme examples. Much more common are actions again showing that what used to be taken for granted as basic civilised behaviour is breaking down. Wirral ambulance vehicles are regularly looted as the crews move from their vehicle into the home of a person requesting emergency help. A service which could not be more obviously run for the immediate needs of citizens is nevertheless considered, by a growing proportion of yobbos, to be fair game.

Undermining authority

The cry which becomes ever more common from my constituents is simply put. Given the collapse of basic decencies we have seen over the past five years alone, what will life be like in ten years' time, let alone when their grandchildren are beginning their own families? And this fear merely assumes the rot continuing at the same rate. In fact, many constituents (and I share this prognosis) see events as showing every sign of accelerating.

Constituents sense that many of the causes of our present discontent are deep-seated and have been building up for many decades. But a single extrapolation of present trends, let alone the nightmare scenario of the whole process gaining greater and greater momentum as it sweeps all before it, signals the urgency of beginning an effective counter-strategy. This new behaviour is bred in families, and it is schools who are increasingly manning the trenches in what is nothing less than a war for civilisation as we know it.

No one should under-rate the pressure many schools are already under. No one is quite sure where Carey is at the moment. She should have been in school but isn't. When she does attend, she and a small band like her, bring a sense of palpable unease to the entire building. A good week for the counter-truant team often results in a bad week for the school.

Carey is looked after by her Nan. Grandparents are increasingly acting as parents, grandparents and foster-parents all rolled into one. The reason why so many nans are becoming parents to their grandchildren is quite simple: drugs, drink or both. And, as is becoming more common, Carey's mum is a drug addict.

As her Nan became older, Carey wrestled out of her control. Slowly Nan's authority was undermined, and there was no one around to help her to repair and strengthen the human dykes which families build to defend civilised behaviour. These defences were simply overwhelmed by Carey's wilful wrongdoing.

The crucial battle Nan lost was to prevent Carey falling in with Jason's gang. She knew the importance of the battle, but was simply no match for it. Carey now chose how she would live her life, when to come in at night, if she would go to school and when she would get blotto with drink.

Death of truth

Maybe twenty-five or so young people are recognisably in the same group of which Carey is now so clearly a part. A big enough group you may say, and the size of an average secondary school class if all of them turned up at once. But the group is small in comparison to the thousand children on the school roll.

The vast majority of the children are normal and a huge credit to themselves and their parents. But just as Carey and her mates are at one extreme, and the majority of normal children at the other, an intermediate group straddles the two. It is here that the battle for civilised values is being fought, and will be lost unless we agree the most radical of changes. This straddling group is on the march and growing.

Truth has already become the major casualty. Much of the middle group still knows what truth is. But Carey and her accomplices, and a growing proportion of this group which straddles the extremes, do not now recognise that there is such a thing as truth. This trend has become much more noticeable over the past five years.

Children have always been good at lying. Likewise, while teachers have always been more than moderately effective in finding out the truth, that task is now growing ever more difficult. The most disturbing aspect of a disturbing trend is that for this growing band the word truth has no objective meaning. Truth is what they say it is. It is nothing more, and it is nothing less.

A Rubicon has already been crossed. The operation of truth depends on a constituency conscious of what it is, and for the whole group being willing to attest that fact. An appeal to a child's instinct that truth is important, once an easy exercise, is now met with a growing sense of incomprehension for many, and by direct hostility from others. Some children still know enough simply to disagree that truth is important. For others such talk might as well be in double Dutch, given the meaning the word purveys.

The death of truth is accompanied by an unwillingness to become involved by decent citizens when their active involvement is needed as a bulwark against any further slide towards a social abyss. This is noticeable not only with the middle group of children straddling the extremes. It is there to be seen amongst that large group of children who are happily well adjusted and are achievers.

Even amongst this group who, not that long ago, could be relied upon not simply to act well themselves, but speak out, and sometimes being more actively involved, there is now a noticeable reluctance to get involved at all. The volunteers to recall events where there has been some kind of trouble are more and more a minority caste. This is itself a sign of these children's lack of confidence to operate fully and openly in our society.

Demise of authority

The death of truth links to a second challenging trend centring around the demise of authority. Society can only function if the rules of the game are accepted and challenged at any one time by only a minority. Some of society's key defences all too soon begin to crack and then crumble if authority is made a constant target. No one group has the time or the energy to rebuff every challenge.

The rules work because they are accepted and are thereby seen to work. But the new nihilists push utilitarianism to the limit. What is the value of that rule or person and what is its value to me now? A total emphasis on 'now' marks another great divide in our society.

Challenging authority by a younger generation is nothing new. What marks out what is happening now is the violence which a growing army of young people, and adults too, use as their weapon. To an increasing extent, authority is conceded only if it can be physically imposed.

Likewise, with respect, which has been hitherto a gentler social binding force than authority. Respect is no longer awarded, or even conceded, simply because a person holds a position.

This collapse of respect is not confined to office holders, such as the monarch or politicians, or to professionals, doctors and teachers for example, but also to the elderly and even from children to their parents.

Respect can still be awarded. The most obvious recent example here has been Princess Diana. While her good work, and general demeanour, won her widespread respect and affection, the awarding of respect to this clearly troubled person has more than a whiff of sulphur about it. What kind of role model does such a troubled figure provide for teenagers and, as importantly, what is the significance of such a choice?

Here and now

Here comes yet another great divide which has already been touched upon – the reign of 'now'. The lack of that social virtue which guarantees the consideration of one's actions over a longer period than simply the present swings into its deadly action. A different mindset reigns. There is only one time span and that is the here and now, and the here and now should provide the biggest possible buzz. A growing group of young people, who consider themselves normal, can see no purpose whatsoever in rules which have been carefully crafted over generations guaranteeing order in the public space. Indeed, in so far as these rules prevent instant buzz and gratification, they are likely to be lashed out against.

Society has become so vulnerable to this attack of the new nihilists partly because the suddenness of the change has not afforded the time to begin constructing adequate defences, let alone examine and remedy the root causes. Once authority worked, and by working no one thought anything more was necessary. By the speed of their surprise attack the new nihilists have shown that authority has no clothes, and stripped of the clothes of respect, authority has all too often been shown to turn quickly and run.

Conclusion

Where is all this bad behaviour going to end up? The new politics challenges both the left and right. The centre-left's belief was that an amelioration of the grosser forms of inequality would speed the march of civilisation. Merely to recite the phrase throws into sharp relief how these idealist hopes have been dashed.

The right stands equally naked before the new politics. Using the full force of the law doesn't work for the simple reason that the law has yet to be fully crafted to counter the new lawlessness. And, at the end of the day, the law cannot keep being pressed into service if voluntary self-control amongst citizens is fast disintegrating.

Seeking legal redress is a sign of just how inadequate and yet how desperate our world now is. Law can only help build the line against a rising tide of disorder. It can punish those who break established rules. It is the most immediate means open to society to protect itself. It can help set against standards of what is acceptable behaviour and what is not. But to be most effective the use of the law has to be backed up by a strategy to teach again all of those social virtues which are central to good and acceptable behaviour.

3. Social virtues and common decencies

Introduction

Government can set the framework in which society's institutions work, but no police force alone is ever going to be effective in enforcing the basic rules of behaviour. That is the task for citizens themselves and was, until very recently, a part of British society which operated so effectively that no-one commented on the success. To remain peaceful, societies over the longer-run have to be self-governing. The three forces which delivered Britain a peaceable kingdom are briefly recalled in this chapter so as to register how big the effort is if we are to build again a successful self-governing community. What was the basis of the self-governing code which is beginning to break down under the onslaught of persistent and widespread anti-social behaviour?

Not by accident alone

The peaceable kingdom which slipped into place with such

apparent ease during the first decades of the 20th century was no accident. It was the product of many forces, of course. But three major events in particular swung into force during the previous hundred years or so, and which above all else forged a public ideology centring on good citizenship. Christianity taught the rudiments of the new belief. Mutual aid ensured that this public ideology ran most of the collective side of public life. The resulting new public ideology's writ then lent support to charitable workers, as well as a growing cadre of public officials, who enforced with greater confidence than they would otherwise have done society's new contract on duties and behaviour. Each of these three fronts divides our society from its immediate past.

Judging behaviour

The collapse of Christian belief has been so swift in the past few decades that it is difficult now to comprehend how prominent it once was. We were a nation of The Book, rather in the way that Muslim countries are today, with the Bible having the minute by minute impact on people's lives as does now the Koran. Here is the first fault line before our own society and what once was.

Yet it is inadequate to explain the shaping of character, which occurred during the nineteenth century as due simply to Christianity. A religion that had prided itself on reserve became, in the main, a religion of practical guidance which was enthusiastically endorsed. This was the age of the evangelical revival, and it permeated practically everywhere.

It was the single most widespread and important influence in Victorian England. More importantly for our story, evangelicalism fed throughout the land to all social groups and, as it spread, it taught a simple, comprehensible public creed of what was expected of everyone. Whilst sincerity was prized, and so too was plain speaking, the central message was that each and everyone would be judged by their character, and that judgement was made on the actions individuals undertook. Moreover, the judgements, once made, were backed up by a comprehensive set of rewards and punishments. Personal responsibility to oneself, family and neighbours were central to this new cosmos.

Paradoxically, just as Christianity was at its zenith in helping shape personal belief into a public ideology, doubt with a capital D began to gain a serious number of adherents. But even those who began to doubt the existence of God believed that it was as vital as ever to teach much of what was Christian morality without God. Any loss of faith was not matched by an equivalent loss of belief in the necessity of the social rules, which Christianity had so effectively imparted, particularly to the nation's young.

Before faith began to ebb, a society was forged believing clearly in what was and was not acceptable behaviour. Now, in contrast, a new breed who doubt the need for an agreed set of positive social rules has been allowed an influence out of all proportion to their numbers, or their worth. The impact on undermining public behaviour of these new doubters' creed cannot be overestimated.

Dominating society

According to the peaceable kingdom's public ideology, how people should live their lives was not a private affair. It dominated how citizens behaved in the public arena. There was a rich public life, but the governance of society had next to nothing to do with the state. Here is the second fault line dividing our own society from a largely self-governing politics.

A huge leap in imagination is again required. The state as we know it today was, even a hundred years ago, not so much unimagined as unimaginable. To us collective action is viewed inevitably as state action. What we find so difficult to comprehend is that not so long ago, collective action was the antithesis of state action. Equally important was that this collective provision taught what the public ideology extolled.

The single most important item in the government's current budget is welfare. It takes a cool third of all taxpayers' money. Welfare was not only once the providence of mutual societies, but that mutual society was both the creation of the public ideology we are discussing, and in return reinforced those collectively held beliefs. In place of the duties by which mutual societies lived, today's welfare centres on rights which have slipped free of the duties which held them socially in check.

The public ideology taught through mutual societies stressed the importance of being responsible personally for one's family, but also for one's neighbour. Today we would say that a social discipline was thereby acquired. But merely to use this phrase highlights how extensive has been the change in our thinking. To our great grandparents behaving well was not the product of social discipline. It was viewed, quite simply, as virtuous behaviour.

Welfare, then as now, is the most important source of income for the vast majority of us outside of work. And, because it plays such an important part in our lives, welfare was used to help shape behaviour. Individuals were not allowed to behave irresponsibly. To allow any individual freedom might endanger the freedom of the majority. The welfare of society has to be protected as well as promoted.

By general consent the practice of virtue, or what was considered good behaviour, was therefore rewarded as its lack was punished. While self-interest reinforced the reward system it also underpinned an effective system of sanctions. If duties were not fully adhered to the rights possessed by each individual were put in jeopardy. Bad behaviour could bring down mutual society on whose existence depended the safe-keeping of what was often decades upon decades of personal savings.

Enforcement officers

An agreed public ideology, which governed public conduct, gave what would now appear to be an unimaginable degree of confidence to those whose role was initiating the young into the wider community. Here then is the third major fault line between that peaceable kingdom and our own society.

Clergy, teachers, police, factory and health inspectors, doctors, and a growing host of other officials, went about their task with assurance. While they would be attending directly to the issues that gave rise to their position – teaching or policing, for example – they knew their work fitted into a much larger picture. They were committed to this wider goal of improving the type of character they and their charges possessed.

This was a view of social advance which is directly at variance to that in which most of us have grown up. Change would come about not by a government decree grandly reordering society's institutions. Change on this scale was never envisaged. It came instead by much more challenging means where changing the values individuals held began to transform society itself. It was not the politics of the elite. This was truly mass politics, even if most of the participants did not then possess the vote.

How we behaved as free citizens was seen to depend on our character. Schools, workplaces, mutual aid bodies and sports clubs were all concerned with raising and strengthening the best side of their members' lives, whether it was by learning, savings or by recreation.

Of course many people fell by the wayside. But many of these were encouraged to rise up again. Likewise, while examples can be cited of brutal teachers, thuggish police officers, careless or corrupt factory inspectors, crooked mutual aid officials, such examples served as a warning, and usually helped to renew the efforts of others to do better.

This great advance which characterised this period was not, of course, beyond criticism. Critics there were and the best pricked the pomposity of the most self-important reformers. Yet despite the mirth so engendered, the nation was not deflected in its main task. A crucial part of the nation's everyday business was about strengthening and transmitting its core values and virtues.

The lessons

What lessons can be usefully drawn from these glimpses of the past? Three are of importance in helping set the new political agenda. First, the kind of people we were, and still are to a large extent, was not the product of chance. The nation came to a mind on how it wanted to live and accepted that such a vision was inseparably bound up with the values individuals and families held.

Second, core values are of little purpose unless they are actively promoted. This was once seen as a task that civil society – church and mutual societies, for example – naturally undertook. We need to gain institutions of similar power and position to undertake this role.

Third, an agreement, and thereby a renewal of society's core values, will achieve more than just giving a clear direction to individuals and families as to what is expected of them. Reaffirming society's core values is the most effective means of strengthening the position of all those individuals who are in positions of authority and, who are, thereby, initiators of the young into society's beliefs about itself.

Christianity is unlikely to play again the role it once did in developing public ideology. The institutions of civil society are only a shadow of what they once were, and currently lack the power to teach in everyday living the personal values of the once all pervasive public ideology. Yet these social virtues, which were extolled and taught so effectively, are the cornerstone of a successful and peaceable society. What specifically are these virtues? That is the question to which we now turn.

The social virtue mix

To live our lives free from unwanted interference from near neighbours has become for each of us a fundamental part of what is regarded in this country as 'the good life'. But 'the good life' did not appear from nowhere. It was very much the product of a group of interlinked social virtues unpinning a sense of common decency.

What are the social virtues which became so well established in this country that their everyday practice helped define universally what constituted civilised behaviour? There are three virtues which I believe are in a league of their own when we are considering what provided the underpinning of common decencies.

The three social virtues which I believe to be premier are politeness, considerateness and thoughtfulness. While each of these virtues is distinct, each touches the other, and the practice of each underpins a sense of common or shared decency. That common decency is born of a recognition that each of us must take on board the needs of other people if, in turn, that response is generally to be reciprocated. Indeed, this response needs to become part of our subconsciousness so that thinking of others automatically affects how we behave. A cornerstone of civilised living has been the development of an innate courtesy which, as the nineteenth century Bishop Francis Paget remarked, consists of the respect of the self-respect of others.

Each of the virtues thereby checks the natural impulses in each of us to please ourselves at the expense of others, whose needs simultaneously have to be met in part if society is to prosper. Individuals lacking these particular virtues cause degrees of aggravation, ranging from simple annoyance at one extreme, right through to a sense of mayhem at the other.

A natural politeness is borne of an attentiveness and respectfulness to the needs of others. Considerateness stems from a generosity of spirit whereby, again, the needs of others who live in close proximity automatically bear on our own behaviour. Likewise, thoughtfulness stems from the ability to read what another person's needs are. A defining characteristic of anti-social individuals stems from their failure to practice any, let alone all three, of the premier social virtues.

The basis of successful reciprocity

William Temple, a wartime Archbishop of Canterbury, observed how once babies begin to observe, they see themselves at the centre of the world. He offered this as a definition of original sin. Whether or not it is sin, original or otherwise, such behaviour is certainly natural. And it is a naturalness that has to be counter-balanced if individuals are to live contentedly alongside each other, and if we are to have a concept of society and not just of self. Teaching how to balance one's own sense of importance with the needs of others has been traditionally one of the more important tasks families undertake.

There has, of course, been something of a pyramid sales operation underlying the continuing operation of these social virtues. Such a sales operation is no bad thing; everybody benefits as long as the pyramid continues to be built. Social virtues are practised because other people practice them. And common decencies became part of our heritage because these social virtues were transmitted from one generation to the next. The sense of crisis, that is only too well expressed today, stems in no small part from an awareness that this gigantic but so beneficial pyramid-type operation is crumbling. As with all such operations, once people's faith is lost the collapse creates a domino effect making further decline inevitable.

Thinking beyond the immediate

Linked to the operation of these three premier social virtues has been the equally important social characteristic whereby individuals think beyond the immediate consequences of their own actions. In many ways this characteristic is the extension of each of the premier social virtues.

If an absence of an ability simultaneously to weigh the needs of others with one's own priorities is the first defining characteristic of anti-social individuals, a second defining characteristic of such individuals and families is that they do not see any value, or relevance, in looking beyond the now in calculating the consequences of their actions. Thinking through the longer-term consequences of their behaviour, both for themselves, and for those with whom they come into contact, is simply an unintelligible activity.

Just as the responsibility for the non-transference of the premier social virtues lies in a dysfunctional family, so the inability or unwillingness of some people to think over the longer-term has been reinforced by a society which guarantees minimum rights and income to individuals almost irrespective of their behaviour.

To take the extreme example, society has, since time immemorial, been organised on the basis that those who are able to work, but refuse to do so, are not fed by the courtesy of other people. This link between personal behaviour and its personal consequences no longer universally applies.

The unconditionality of much welfare, for example, has severed the connection between a person's actions and accepting the consequences of that pattern of behaviour. How best to re-link individual action to the consequences of that action for the individual concerned, and to do so in an age of human rights, is one of the challenges examined in the latter part of the book.

Conclusion

There is no time machine into which we can slip and move back to a society which once existed. But to glimpse over our shoulder shows how significant a change there must be to current politics if anti-social behaviour is to be successfully countered. Society needs to agree once again upon what type of people we as citizens should be. Crucial here are the premier social virtues we practice in our lives. Politeness, considerateness and thoughtfulness did not simply appear out of the air, or even tumble down Mount Sinai. Nor were they simply taught by rote to successive generations of compliant youths. A largely self-governing society developed these values which automatically guided behaviour and instilled the idea that living for the moment did not lay the basis for long-term happiness. This society also devised a range of rewards and punishments to protect this common culture.

Changing politics so that we can consider the best means for teaching these values, and how the resulting public ideology can best be reflected in public institutions, is not for anyone believing in a quick fix. None of these objectives will be achieved without a determined effort. We must now turn to begin thinking about the moves back to a more peaceable kingdom. To begin this task we need first to consider what is new about anti-social behaviour.

4. What is special about anti-social behaviour?

Introduction

How best to counter anti-social behaviour is one of the major issues facing the government. But how should anti-social behaviour be defined? Currently the public debate is being conducted as though practically all public disorders are manifestations of anti-social behaviour. One reason for this is that with the police being so stretched, the easy get out is to define all disorder not dealt with adequately as anti-social behaviour. Such loose talk not only makes the immediate task politically unmanageable, but it misses the one aspect of anti-social behaviour which makes the current situation so challenging. Anti-social behaviour isn't a new form of criminal behaviour. Rather it springs from acts of annoyance being committed so repetitively that a new and understandable grievance is registered by those on the receiving end of such actions. These acts of gross annoyance arise because indi-

vidual behaviour is not restrained by what I have just defined as those premier social virtues, or common decencies, which safeguard the dignity of other people. Here we consider how best to concentrate on what is new about today's disorder.

Road blocks in the way to understanding

There are two significant road blocks obstructing the roll-out of an effective anti-social behaviour strategy. The first one arises from the lack of an agreement on what constitutes anti-social behaviour. The second stems from a fundamental disagreement as to the root causes of this kind of behaviour.

What constitutes anti-social behaviour is clearly part of the law and order debate. But anti-social behaviour does not produce an indentikit picture of the breaking of civil and criminal law. Some anti-social behaviour is undertaken by individuals who are also criminals. Some individuals who behave in an anti-social manner, many perhaps, will become criminals if their behaviour goes unchecked. But what the public and the politicians are trying to grapple with here is a new phenomena, at least in recent times.

Making the present system work better

Being clear on what is and what is not anti-social behaviour will help push to one side the first road block to a successful strategy. This is not a simple semantic argument. Making anti-social behaviour a catch-all definition, covering all kinds of disturbance, leads to an almost equally unfocussed response.

It is already clear that anti-social behaviour presents a serious challenge for citizens and the government alike. Countering such behaviour will require imagination and staying power. Moreover, building a counter-strategy is going to be difficult enough without categorising every kind of disorder as anti-social behaviour. It is crucial to focus on those unacceptable public activities for which there is no, or, so far, only an inadequate antidote.

Some of what is termed anti-social behaviour, particularly that by adults, can be dealt with under existing law, and should be dealt with accordingly. As well as possibly bringing some immediate redress, such an approach will raise three immediate challenges which must then become part of the political debate on law and order, as well as anti-social behaviour.

Delays getting into court

The first challenge concerns the length of time it takes to get cases into court to counter criminal and civil violation of the law, and, in particular, bringing into play existing powers to counter disorder. How to bring cases of violent disorder before the court, within days after clear warnings have been issued to cease behaving so offensively, must be an objective the government should pursue with imagination and determination.

Here is one example which is not, sadly, untypical of the length of time it took Wirral Council to move through the courts to seek an eviction for one of those infamous 'neighbours from hell'. The tenant was accused of letting her children run wild, their targeting of neighbouring pensioners, and the slashing of car tyres, as well as threats being made to neighbours by her boyfriend. This tenant was in clear breach of her tenancy agreement.

Those neighbours who lodged the complaint were requested to keep diaries detailing the nature and frequency of their complaints over a number of months. The council issued a couple of warnings requesting a change in behaviour. Failure on this score led the council to seek an eviction order.

Wirral's neighbour nuisance team applied to the court for the tenant's eviction in December 2000 and the first hearing was listed for February the following year. At this hearing a trial date was set for June 2001. Not until the actual date of the trial did the defendant submit a doctor's note asserting that the defendant was unwell. The trial was adjourned until September. On the day of the trial the defendant submitted a doctor's note again alleging ill health preventing her from attending the court. This time the court decided to proceed and granted an eviction.

The court process alone took ten months, but it was well over a year after the first official complaint was lodged with the council for the tenant to be evicted, during which time the anti-social behaviour continued unabated. And this timescale fails to include the lengthy period of time neighbours put up with and tried to change the behaviour of this family before they sought the council's help. Once evicted, the tenant then made off to the private sector where she was free to begin her reign of terror on a new set of unsuspecting neighbours.

An adequate police budget

A second challenge will arise from using existing powers to the full in countering disorder. Such a strategy will bring into sight the question many senior politicians appear least anxious to discuss: is the law and order budget anywhere near adequate? At the moment the catch-all approach to anti-social behaviour acts as a very convenient decoy.

Much of the current disorder could and should be countered by using appropriately and effectively the existing criminal and civil law. But for this objective to be realised the police need substantially greater resources. Instead of opening up this debate on how serious the shortfall of personnel is, chief constables are, if not prime drivers, willing accomplices in trying to close down the debate on why existing laws are not enforced robustly.

The unspecified nature of anti-social behaviour is used as a cover for a wider failure in policing. While this line gives senior police chiefs and politicians respite, that comfort is not afforded to the poor punters who are left bewildered at the failure to devise a counter-strategy to the new disorder.

The issue of an adequate police budget must be confronted. Beyond question, the government is right to seek by all legitimate means the best use of existing police resources. At the same time, the question has to be asked what magnitude of increased resources is required before the police offer a uniform service against crime as well as anti-social behaviour throughout the country.

Any significant increase in resources will have to be built up over time to ensure the right people can be recruited and best use is made of taxpayers' money. Can the police force achieve a uniformly first class service throughout the country with less than a fifty per cent rise in the law and order budget? I doubt it. How that extra money might be raised is considered in the final chapter.

The issue, of course, is not simply one of money. How much more imaginatively any level of resources could be used is also a key part of the debate. But I do not believe major inroads can be made against the current level of disorder without a significant increase in resources spent by the community to maintain order. The increased cost to the taxpayer will not stop with the law and order budget, of course. As well as ensuring the line against disorder is more firmly held, the larger part of an effective counter-strategy has to go to what might crudely be termed as cutting supply routes to anti-social behaviour.

Destruction of businesses

I am writing to see if you could find out what is happening to a Public House which I work very close to. It is called the Signet and is on the corner of Watson Street and St Anne Street, Birkenhead.

When the resident landlord left last year a temporary manager was appointed. She stayed a couple of weeks and left. The pub was left empty till they appointed a new manager. But before he could take over it was set on fire. Since then it has been left for the vandals and local drug addicts to destroy. It has been flooded out and set alight again. Youths climb on the flat part of the roof drinking alcohol then throw the empty bottles down to the ground regardless of who may be passing below. Also tiles have been taken from the roof and thrown to the ground. The police don't come any more as they say they haven't the manpower. Even when they did, the vandals had gone before they arrived.

Since the pub closed last year local businesses have suffered greatly. The local Post Office was closed causing hardship to the old and disabled people in the area. The chemist is closing shortly and the local convenience store is being forced to close, not all through the vandals but through the lack of business as people don't come to St Anne Street like they used to.

The people who own the pub, Enterprise Inns, have done little or nothing to keep the building in a good state of repair, or get it up and running as a going public house, and it was twelve months ago. Their reluctance to sell the property and lack of security of the building has brought about a general decline in the area.

I have the names of four people who have put in genuine offers for the pub who would repair it and get it up and running again. But Enterprise has declined their offers. Surely they can be forced to sell, or repair and make safe the building?

A constituent from Birkenhead

Balancing justice towards the innocent

The third challenge arises from the law favouring the guilty. The question my constituents pose, and answer in the negative, I have to add, is whether the balance between the rights of those who cause disorder, and the rights of those against whom the disorder is aimed, is now fairly drawn. In particular it is urgent to look at how the European Convention on Human Rights, itself a convention of noble intent, sometimes works unjustifiably to protect the recidivist anti-social behaviourists.

In Britain, a select committee of Lords and Commons has a duty to review all proposed legislation to see if it is compatible with the Convention. Reading the committee reports suggests an approach to countering disorder that is widely at variance with what voters register as fair. Here are a few examples of the committee's thinking, which are valuable as they illustrate its dominant attitude to legislative reform which must be challenged if the law is to be an effective agent against anti-social behaviour.

In 2001 the committee examined the clauses in what became the Criminal Justice Act. The proposal to make a new offence of bar staff permitting drunkenness was judged as likely to compromise the bar staff's right to freedom of expression. On child curfew proposals the committee accepted, on balance, that this proposal was in the public interest but tempered this judgement by declaring that these powers could be used in a disproportionate way. This judgment could not have been wider of the mark. Not a single child curfew order has yet been issued anywhere in Great Britain.

There is only a single exception where championing of individual rights over the rights of the majority does not take precedence. This came with the committee's review, also in 2001 of the Hunting Bill, which had the aim of forbidding hunting with dogs.

Article 1 of the Convention gives a clear right to the 'quiet enjoyment of (the) ownership of property' and the Committee viewed that hunting on one's own land would be covered by this provision. It then added that a deprivation of such a right could be enforced if it is in the public interest, a stance that is rarely struck on issues trying to deal with anti-social behaviour.

The committee's lack of balance was again displayed when it reported on the Housing Benefit (Withholding of Payment) Bill. Any family losing their right to housing benefit would only do so after the courts had twice judged against them. Yet to checkmate this move the committee cited Article 3 of the Convention on the right of such families not to be subjected to degrading treatment, adding that such protection was absolute. No such protection against degrading treatment it would appear is offered by the Convention, or by the committee's deliberations, to families on the receiving end of gross anti-social behaviour.

In a further argument against the Bill, the committee cited how a child's education and social life may be disrupted by homelessness and a need to move to a different area. The weight of opinion was once again swung in defence of unacceptable behaviour.

No mention here of why a child might have to move to a different area. Nor was there even a hint of a child's right to be brought up in a safe environment and to be taught by his or her parents the basic social skills necessary to be an adequate, let alone an exemplary citizen.

Each of these three challenges – the time it takes to get to court and for justice to be seen working, the level of resources needed by the police to give a first class service, and the balance of the law weighted in favour of the lawbreaker – is considered in the final section of this volume. Action along these fronts will form a key part of any strategy to counter the level of disorder in our society. But such action will not by itself form a comprehensive attack on anti-social behaviour. For success here we must also single out what is new about those actions which ride under the title of anti-social behaviour.

A new definition

Using existing powers fully against those committing disorder does not need to wait for the formulation of a working definition of anti-social behaviour. But such a definition is urgent if further counter-measures are to be judged effectively. What is required is to gain an accurate picture in words of what anti-social behaviour is in practice.

I single out as a prime example here the definition given by the Scottish Office on anti-social behaviour. I do so not because the

Scottish Office's approach is less clear than any other definition that has been put forward by official bodies. Far from it. The Scottish Office, in fact, has been one of the most thoughtful and proactive institutions on this whole issue. It is, rather, that we now need to move swiftly beyond what has been offered so far as a working definition so as to focus much more sharply on what the political response should be in the largely new territory in which we now find ourselves.

The Scottish Office has described anti-social behaviour as taking on many different forms with varying levels of intensity. 'It can include vandalism, noise, verbal and physical abuse, threats of violence, racial harassment, damage to property, trespass, nuisance from dogs, car repairs on the street, joy-riding, domestic violence, drugs and other criminal activities such as house-breaking' or examples of the breaking of one or more aspects of the existing law.

The omnibus nature of the most currently used definitions of anti-social behaviour works against devising a clear action plan. The canvas is drawn so widely that it is nearly impossible to focus clearly on what is happening. A workable definition of anti-social behaviour has to alight first on the relative newness of much of what is now happening. Much of today's unacceptable behaviour is of a different order to what preceded it and, because it is new, effective means of dealing with it have generally still to be devised. Equally important, if any long-term strategy is to be effective, the root causes of anti-social behaviour have to be located.

I see anti-social behaviour as due to the collapse in the standards of personal behaviour which awards due respect for another human being. Practically all criminal and many civil misdeeds, of course, share this characteristic and, as I keep arguing, such actions should be countered by the existing law. In contrast, the distinguishing mark of anti-social behaviour is that each single instance does not by itself warrant a counter legal challenge. It is in its regularity that anti-social behaviour wields its destructive force. It is from the repetitive nature of the nuisance that anti-social behaviour is born.

It is because such behaviour was, until quite recently, unimaginable that no effective legal remedy exists to counter it, although a start has been made with various anti-social behaviour orders. It is this lack of effective and comprehensive redress that largely accounts for anti-social behaviour being seen as one facet of the rise in crime or, almost as importantly, the fear of crime and disorder.

The second road block to success

The basis of the second road block is the fundamental disagreement on the root causes of anti-social behaviour. There is a powerful lobby who hold what has become the traditional left view on unacceptable behaviour. Anti-social behaviour is primarily a form of protest. Here the root cause of such behaviour is seen as stemming from the unfairness and injustices in our society against which individuals naturally rail. Remove the injustices and, hey presto, behaviour changes, or so the story goes.

On this count, anti-social behaviour is merely the outward visible sign of a society which treats some individuals so badly that, instead of rioting in a traditional manner, the aggrieved individuals develop a whole series of low burn acts of rebellion. Clearly some people's behaviour is affected by their feelings that 'the system' has dealt them a pretty miserable hand. But this analysis of anti-social behaviour is largely mistaken.

Much of the unacceptable behaviour is caused, less by any sense of rising up against injustice, than by human nature reacting as it will when there is no clear framework within which it should operate. Injustices should be tackled, but it would be wrong to think that such reforms will of themselves counter anti-social behaviour.

Another group, led by the Prime Minister, rejects this basically Utopian belief about how human nature behaves in adversity. The concern of this group of politicians, understandably enough, given the growing sense of crisis, is to mobilise public support for an expanding array of sanctions against their perpetrators of disorder. Since 1997 the government has initiated an impressive number of counter-poverty measures. A raft of tax credits and Sure Start programmes are only two such initiatives.

The Prime Minister and his allies believe that individuals should maximise these new opportunities presented to them. More importantly, should these individuals decide not to, and behave instead in an unacceptable manner in public, the government's anti-poverty strategy secures for the Administration a moral authority to crack down on such disorder.

There can be no doubt that some offending and offensive individuals will respond in the way the government believes. But to believe that this opportunity strategy, backed up with no-nonsense anti-social behaviour and acceptable behaviour contracts will, given time, re-establish the world we are fast losing is too optimistic. As I have argued, *Neighbours from Hell* sees anti-social behaviour as being caused by much more fundamental changes in society.

Losing the battle

Anti-social behaviour stems from the breakdown of a public ideology which centred on promoting a sense of common decency. This breakdown has allowed the rise of dysfunctional families who fail to teach their children those personal virtues which are crucial to establishing common decencies. It is because the root cause lies here that we see a growing number of children coming to school with little or no idea of how to behave. Likewise, the gangs that maraud around the streets inflicting fear and much destruction, are not urban guerrillas fighting for justice, but semi-barbaric youths who have scant, or no respect for the dignity of others.

Chapter two tried to give some idea of how far the new behaviour has advanced. I drew on my experience as a constituency MP in Birkenhead for more than two decades to illustrate the forces giving rise to the new politics. Any number of examples of the collapse of decent behaviour could have been given. No school is totally exempt from its impact. Few working class areas are untouched. Many public workers bear more than the brunt of this new barbarism as they go about their business. And this is as true generally for the country as a whole as it is for Birkenhead.

This war continues to rage with no sight of its abatement. Indeed, most of the indications point to a failure to hold the line. Most worrying of all is the change in attitudes to this war from those who, until recently, would have been volunteers in defence of decent behaviour. A growing proportion of this group now opts for non-combat roles. Disengagement is becoming the order of the day. We shall need to examine more fully the root causes of anti-social behaviour as the discussion turns to building up a comprehensive counter-strategy.

Conclusion

Crime and disorder compete for the top slot in public attention. The failure to deal more effectively with the breaking of the civil and criminal law is in part due to the inadequacy of police resources in comparison with the size of the task. This failure is not confronted. A sticky veil of 'anti-social behaviour' is thrown over the whole issue, partly because the most senior of police officers are afraid to break rank and tell the public as it is. But this response of trying to deflect attention leaves the punters in deep puzzlement as they are only too well aware of what anti-social behaviour is. Everybody knows that something significant is happening, but at this point agreement ends.

The root cause of anti-social behaviour is a direct result of the failure of families to pass on to their offspring what I have called the fundamental or premier social virtues. A small and growing number of families have become dysfunctional in this most important respect. This dysfunctionalism would have at one time been checked by a public confidence in enforcing a set of common decencies. That confidence by the main agents in setting public standards of behaviour is fracturing. Linked to, and reinforcing the absence of, virtuous behaviour is a growing inability by some individuals to think through the longer-term consequences of their actions.

The behaviour of this dysfunctional minority is but an extreme example of a trend working through most of British society. There has been a significant shift overall in the regard individuals have for one another. A fully effective reform programme has to deal with these wider changes, as well as the more immediate challenge thrown up by a minority of families. How to respond effectively is the basis of the new politics.

5. Political virtue

Introduction

For thousands of years politics addressed one of the most fundamental of all questions. Never far from the centre of political thinking was the question 'what kind of people do we want ourselves and our fellow citizens to be?' It is a very recent development which sees political activity mainly in terms of managing the market, although this objective is clearly important. While it is now urgent to take politics back to the basic question of what kind of people should we aim to be, opposition to such a political strategy is likely to be considerable.

Advent of modern politics

In the summer months of 2002 I introduced a parliamentary bill to withdraw housing benefit from 'neighbours from hell.' Although the bill was defeated under the time rules, debating withdrawing housing benefit offered a major advantage: it was during these debates that the most likely arguments against the new politics were given their first outing. As opponents will no doubt deploy each of these contentions as the curtain goes up big time on the new politics, it is important to review and evaluate each one. They can best be grouped under five headings.

Broken-backed government

The first two objections feature in the 'can't do, won't do' lexicon of political inactivity. The arguments refer, in the first instance, to a belief that even if the approach of *Neighbours from Hell* was desirable, changing behaviour for the better is beyond the power of government. Indeed, it is alleged, there is already a major crisis of confidence amongst the public who see a government well able to announce initiatives, but which does not have the powers or ability to see policies taken through to a successful conclusion.

Government initiatives, to be sure, are announced, and hardly a day goes by without one or even a clutch of such initiatives being spun from the recesses of Downing Street. But seeing these initiatives through to a successful conclusion, which is what the voters want, is a totally different matter. The age of big government is over. This approach is best summarised as government in retreat.

The present collapse in the belief that governments can deliver has its roots in an earlier part of the post-war period. Two events helped shape the views of the silent majority. The first comes from voters witnessing what was euphemistically called withdrawal from empire. The sight of successive governments being pushed out of our colonial territories, usually after a failure to counter terrorist activities, entered the British psyche. If one of the great powers, for that is how we saw ourselves then, was forced on to the run, what hope could there be for governments to tackle issues directly on the home front?

The other major failure of government was wholly domestic. As unemployment began what then appeared to be its inexorable rise, governments of both parties preached Keynesianism, but the voters saw the tide of unemployment rise to even higher peaks over each successive economic cycle. Could there be a larger or more important example of the failure of government? This is the rhetorical question posed by proponents of this argument.

But was the failure to deal effectively with unemployment an example of government being unable to deliver on an issue of most concern to the electorate, or was it yet another example of big government failing to deliver because they were following the wrong policies? Looking back on this period we witness successive governments applying Keynesian reflationary measures as the economy went into recession, although prices were rising and the reflationary measures simply added further to the inflationary pressures which were themselves the main destroyers of jobs.

Since the last recession, in the very early 1990's, a combination of appropriate fiscal and monetary policy has delivered the longest post-war boom, the longest sustained period of economic growth, and a record creation of 3.1 million jobs in the British economy since the final quarter of 1992, the low point of employment during the early 1990s recession. Of this total, 1.5 million jobs have been created since Labour came to power in May 1997. But public perceptions of past government actions remain. The economic woes of the 1960s and 1970s have left a deep sediment of government failure across the public consciousness.

Government action by itself doesn't guarantee success. But the often embellished media picture of somewhat frantic Ministers, wild-eyed, manically pulling lever after lever on which the word power is inscribed, only to find that the levers are unconnected to anything, is simply a caricature wheeled out by reporters as a substitute for careful thinking and analysis.

There are a whole series of examples where governments over the past twenty years have been successful in delivering on their objectives. The most important Thatcher achievement was to bring trade unions within the law as the government defined it, rather than allowing trade union leaders to define the law within which they would conduct their activities. Right up to the point of success, critics, even within her own government, were whispering to the media how this strategy would fail. Similarly, the second Thatcher administration, in particular, could point to a record of achievement in pushing through an extensive privatisation programme.

More recent success can be reported on raising basic literacy and numeracy standards in primary schools. The current government can also point to an important promise fulfilled with respect to devolution for Scotland and Wales. Likewise, this is the first Labour government not to tip the economy into crisis.

A no entry sign

The second and linked counter-blast against the new politics sees opponents smartly jumping from what is an essentially empirical objection – government can't perform – to an attempt to occupy the moral high ground. Behaviour is a no-go area for government activity, comes the quick retort.

Even if governments could change behaviour for the better, this objective could only be achieved by the state pushing its sticky fingers into people's private lives, and this is not a legitimate activity. The attempt by critics to occupy the high ground is misplaced, for, although the new politics is different, it is most definitely not about invading the private, as opposed to trying to influence what goes on in the public domain.

Keeping government out of the private lives of the citizenry is laudable and has deep roots in our political culture. It was possibly expressed most poetically by Elizabeth I when she declared her opposition to opening windows into men's souls. Men and women's souls remain outside the ambit of democratic politics. But, it is instructive to consider the background to the Good Queen's utterance of this remarkable phrase, for it makes a fundamental distinction which takes us to the centre point of the new politics.

Then, and what is again an urgent requirement, a new contract was being established between the Crown and its subjects, and this contract was based on reciprocity. As part of the agreement she struck with her subjects, the first Elizabeth was concerned not to be seen prying into the religious beliefs of those subjects who held views outside the compass of what is now known as the Anglican settlement. But this liberty was only granted to those who held other beliefs, so long as the holding of such beliefs did not disturb the public peace. This was the rub, or the reciprocity.

Similarly, at no point is the aim of *Neighbours from Hell* to open a window or anything else into the minds, thoughts or beliefs of voters. Everyone has a right to hold whatever views they wish. We enter into a different realm, however, when these private views are expressed in public.

Once in the public arena private views, by definition, remain no longer private. Private opinions are usually made public with one objective. They are offered in the hope or determination to change the views of other people. Once such opinions are made regularly in a concerted manner in public, the guardians of our public space have a responsibility to consider the impact on the public peace of making private views public.

As with private opinions, so too, with respect to values that determine behaviour. Once those values determining conduct are operating in the public domain, they cease to be a private concern only, and become part of the stuff of politics.

The discussion is therefore turned back to the central conviction of *Neighbours from Hell*. If the new politics can be said to be about anything, it is on how best to challenge the private views and values which are impacting so adversely on public conduct. In no way is *Neighbours from Hell* advocating some kind of thought police. The new politics only sees social virtues as a political issue, with these virtues becoming a part of an emerging political agenda, because their failure to be transmitted from one generation to another is having the most dire consequences on public behaviour.

The underpinning of our common decencies is fracturing and continues to be further undermined. The teaching of those cardinal values, which instil a degree of thoughtfulness for other people, is now pivotal to a decent life as we know it. The lack of a shared common decency is a public issue as the lack of thoughtfulness for other people boomerangs back into private lives, so reinforcing an already destructive trend. It is when the private impinges so immediately on the public that politics comes into play.

Can't make people good

A third objection centres on what is likely to become a mantra played at an ever increasing volume, namely, that the law or politics cannot make people good. It is true that politics are ineffective if they try to compel a populace to fulfil what is generally regarded by most of them as the 'good life'. But that is not the same as arguing that we do not have a duty to try and prevent, and if we fail, to punish those breaking the minimum rules necessary so that others can strive for that good life. To think otherwise is a fairly recent phenomenon.

Politics has invariably been concerned with such issues. Anyone who holds any doubt here need only look at this country's statute book to see that truth lies in the opposite direction. It is a legitimate area of politics to reaffirm society's basic rules, if necessary by sanctions, while simultaneously trying to help citizens to pursue the good life by every non-coercive means at society's disposal.

Here then is a crucial difference in the style of the new politics. It will be important for the political practitioner to keep in mind a division between moral aspirations – such as striving towards the good life – and a moral duty – such as bringing up one's children to respect other people.

To fail to reach the first is a shortcoming. It is not a wrongdoing, and failure here should not carry any punishment, although society may seek to employ every incentive as its disposal to achieve such an objective. Moral or civic duties, on the other hand, provide the very foundations upon which civilised life is built, and are a proper area for legislative prescription and, if necessary, for sanctions.

Thatcher's ghost

A fourth objection will be played out subliminally. Mrs T's shadow still stretches across our politics. While it is well over a decade since she was tipped out of Downing Street, voters and politicians alike are generally divided into two main camps in their views on an individual who, I believe, will rate as one of the major political figures in Britain of the last 100 years.

What the new politics is will have to be spelt out carefully if the Thatcher factor is not to play what can be only a negative role. A large section of the public see Thatcherism primarily in terms of an attack on the public and an elevation of the private, no matter what the costs or the circumstances of doing so. Opponents of the new politics will try and harness this anti-Thatcher feeling by suggesting that here is Thatcherism again emphasising the individual over the collective.

Neighbours from Hell moves the debate on. Its central message is that increasingly there will be less and less of the collective (society) if we do not take seriously how individuals and families carry out a primary responsibility to teach the basis of common decencies. How accurate the indictment is, that Thatcherism was simply about exalting the private, can be left for a leisurely debate for others to conduct. I simply add that, to me, Mrs Thatcher's almost pathological drive to centralise to herself as many decisions as possible sits uncomfortably with the critics' view that her stewardship was a backward charge into a laissez faire night-watchman state.

But even assuming it was true that Thatcherism was only about transferring responsibilities from the state to the individual, it is a fallacy to argue that any emphasis on individual duties amounts to a resurrection of Thatcherism. Long before now I hope the reader has sympathised with *Neighbours from Hell*'s central proposition, that society as we have known it cannot survive unless we now take seriously the task of strengthening and rebuilding the basis of a shared culture based on common decencies.

This is a new debate that in no way constitutes a rehash of those old disputes which so dominated the 1980s. Fencing with the powerful shadow of Mrs T should cease if we are to try to change events with anything like the determination that she displayed.

Irresponsible landlords

I realise that one must not be over-censorious, especially in an area like the Rhondda, the economic raison d'etre for which more or less vanished a generation ago, with the closure of pits and shutdown of heavy industry. At the same time, I cannot help noticing that my neighbours on either side in this street one of whom is the serial-criminal addressee of the Pontypridd County Court judgement in my favour last year, and both of whom I know to be tenants of the same publicly-subsidised 'housing benefit' landlord, who has not even troubled to hide her anxiety to acquire my house to complete her 'portfolio' are able to afford motor cars and satellite television, as well as a total of twelve illegitimate children, whilst I cannot even run to a terrestrial television licence.

The 'politics of envy' are distasteful and run counter to the sort of Christian virtues so admirably espoused by our inspiring Archbishop... But I do agree that there ought to be some sort of social quid pro quo for state benefits, if only because my neighbours so perfectly illustrate the old adage about the work Satan makes for idle hands. I have reservations, I must say, about your* suggestions for taking away child benefit. Having borne five children of my own, I feel only pity for the little mites, even when (as here) they are encouraged by feckless parents who in turn are being egged on by Rachmannite landlords, to indulge in the sort of petty harassments which go to make everyday life intolerable for elderly people. In a situation like mine, it is the landlords who need to be hit in the pockets which are all they are bothered about. I don't know whether you realise this, but in this street houses which cost less than £10K command annual Housing Benefit rentals, entirely paid for by the Exchequer, of £4k. Such economics positively invite harassment of respectable elderly owner-occupiers.

A South Wales pensioner

* It was in fact the Prime Minister's suggestion.

Bashing the poor

A last major assault on *Neighbours from Hell* is most likely to wear the disguise that the new politics is nothing more than an attack on the poor themselves. As this line is likely to feature prominently in the ensuing debate, the data we have on whose quality of life is most reduced by anti-social behaviour is considered in the next chapter, where the views of poor people themselves will be brought in to centre stage. Here it is important to examine the antecedents of the counter argument, which will no doubt be spun into the public debate.

Deep emotions will be stirred as opponents try to entrench themselves into what they see as the post-war poverty consensus. The liberation from the Victorian approach – or so it is interpreted –

came when the poverty debate began laying the blame for poverty on society and its institutions, instead of the poor themselves. Gone was the age of blaming the victim for their poverty.

Likewise, the more recently established conventional wisdom is that poverty is caused by lack of money and not by the behaviour of the poor themselves. If there is a question to ask about their behaviour this is viewed in social work parlance as a 'presenting problem', presenting a lack of money as the root cause of dysfunctionalism.

The truth is, of course, that each of these beliefs or assertions gives only a partial view of poverty. Poverty is clearly caused by a lack of money, but the expenditure patterns of some of the poor – just like the rich – leave much to be desired. But, likewise, why is it that some poor people manage their finances in a way that puts the budgeting of other classes to shame?

Similarly, how society organises itself can be a cause of poverty. Not to have an adequate minimum retirement pension covering everyone is the major cause of poverty in old age. A clear example, one might say, of what is referred to as institutional poverty. But reflect further.

Some retired people who were on low income for all or most of their working lives not only saved for their retirement, but did so to a degree that took them off welfare. At the same time, other pensioners who during their working lives had a similar income saved next to nothing. How can these different circumstances be explained if personal character, and its view of responsibility, is written out of the script?

To assert that the offending individuals and families have to take responsibility for their own actions will nevertheless, sadly, be labelled by opponents as yet another example of the 'blaming the poor' syndrome merely dressed in a new suit of clothes. Such a label will not stand up to serious scrutiny. The plain and simple fact is that it invariably is poorer people who are the most vociferous in calling for action to be taken against bad behaviour.

The reason for this is very simple, and the next chapter examines the evidence so far published on to whom and in which areas the plague of anti-social behaviour has descended. This review shows clearly that it is the working class and poor who are the worst affected groups of the population. Here all that remains to be done is to tease out what is really being said when opponents will not seriously consider the issue and attempt to disrupt debate with such pavlovian responses as 'it is an attack on the poor'.

Conclusion

The main arguments against looking to politics to begin answering the question as to what kind of people we want citizens to be do not carry much weight. The need to ask this question does not stem from a mindless wish to recruit the nation into an army meddling in other people's business.

The new politics emerges from necessity. A small but growing number of dysfunctional families fail to transmit those social virtues essential to public well-being. This failure to relay the basis of common decency is becoming more, not less, of a problem, and is endangering an ever-growing proportion of the population.

Hence the relevance of the observation by the American academic turned diplomat and politician, Daniel Moynihan. Reviewing his career, Moynihan commented 'I have served in the cabinet or sub-cabinet of four Presidents. I do not believe I have ever heard at a cabinet meeting a serious discussion . . . concerned with how men rather than markets behave. These are necessary first questions of government'. One reason why the new politics is beginning to command an ever-greater billing is that, when in government, people of Moynihan's views and insight did little – nothing it appears in Moynihan's case – to steer colleagues' conversations in a more positive direction.

Before considering the form that discussion should take, what official data there is on anti-social behaviour is reviewed. This shows not only that anti-social behaviour is rising steeply, but that it occurs most frequently in poorer areas. Far from the new politics being an attack on the poor, it is an exercise in reprioritising one of the issues which affects most cruelly the poor themselves.

6. It's the poor, stupid!

Introduction

One of the charges that has already been levelled against Neighbours from Hell *is that it constitutes a new form of poor-baiting, explaining away deep-seated societal problems by blaming the poor for their own misfortunes. But politicians in touch with their constituents know that it is from working class and poorer people themselves that the most forceful pleas come for controlling the behaviour of that as yet small minority who make their neighbours' lives such a misery. The reason for the force of this plea, and its source, is simple. Here we review those national surveys which show that the poorer an area is, the worse is the anti-social behaviour.*

Horsemen of the Apocalypse

Whatever picture the official crime statistics now paint of falling crime rates, a growing proportion of the population believe crime is increasing. They feel a heightened sense of disorder and that, as a consequence, they are unsafe. These perceptions, however, are not spread evenly around the country. The surveys report some people suffering disproportionately.

Two key sets of data help answer the question as to who these people are. The first draws on single studies, often centring on other issues such as hard to let housing, which also record the extent of anti-social behaviour, and who is most affected by it. The second set of material comes from detailed questions in the regular British Crime Survey (BCS) asking specifically about anti-social behaviour. What pattern emerges from these two sets of data about who is most likely to report that anti-social behaviour adversely affects the quality of their life?

Crime, disorder and anti-social behaviour are now the horsemen of the apocalypse. While well capable of acting on their own, these horsemen are more commonly seen riding over the same territory in joint attacks on homes, vehicles and people, so adding enormously to a prevailing sense of unease which often tips into fear and despair. Anti-social behaviour is important because it is the newest horseman of the apocalypse.

It is also important because it thrives most easily in areas where the other apocalypse riders so frequently plunder. Anti-social behaviour then returns the compliment; left unchecked, it provides an easy recruiting ground for the other two, longer-established riders. Anti-social behaviour therefore needs to be set against the traditional pattern of crime and disorder, in order to appreciate the extent to which the newest apocalypse rider also disproportionately directs his attention to poorer people living in the poorest areas.

Patterns of burglary, violence and vehicle crime

First, then, the pattern of crime for burglary, vehicles and violence. National housing data shows that the poorest people are generally tenants in the socially rented sector – local authority and housing association accommodation. All the available data details with monotonous repetition crime rates being at least twice as high in these poor areas than elsewhere.

A person living in the socially rented sector, for example, is twice as likely to be the victim of a burglary than as is an owner occupier. Homes on council estates are twice as likely to be burgled than other dwellings. Households where the head is unemployed experience twice the rate of burglaries than households where the head is in work.

Social renters are much more likely to be the victims of theft of, or from, a vehicle than are home owners. Similarly, residents of flats or maisonettes (types of accommodation much more likely to be found in the socially rented sector) are twice as likely to be the victims of vehicle related offences than residents of detached properties.

Acts of violence record a similar pattern. Over 8 per cent of unemployed people responding to the latest BCS had been a victim of violence during 1999 or 2000. Just over 5 per cent of respondents living in council estates had physical injuries inflicted on them in this way. This 8 and 5 per cent respectively needs to be noted against a national benchmark of 3.7 per cent of respondents reporting acts of violence against their person.

This national benchmark has, of course, been pushed up because of inclusion of working class areas. So outside working class areas the level of violence against the person is generally significantly lower than the national average.

On each of these three fronts then – being a victim of burglary, being on the receiving end of a vehicle related crime, or being a victim of violence – people living in inner-cities, and other similar poorer areas, bear more than their fair share of crime, and that is why the demand in chapter four to increase significantly the active police force is important in countering effectively this tide of crime which affects the poor and working class most.

If there is any issue which still divides along the old class lines it is crime. If we now turn our attention to where anti-social behaviour is most likely to occur, we see a similar pattern emerging as to that on crime and disorder.

Patterns of anti-social behaviour

While anti-social behaviour has only recently begun to register in public debate, there has been over the past five years a growing number of surveys suggesting that anti-social behaviour is worst in the poorest areas; that residents in such areas link disorder and anti-social behaviour together; that once anti-social behaviour becomes part of the scene, those people who can get out of the area do so as quickly as possible, thereby adding considerably to the sense of unease in those areas; and that ever more time is spent by officials trying to counter the worst effects of anti-social behaviour.

As with crime and disorder, anti-social behaviour does not fall evenly as does God's gentle rain. It strikes most frequently at the highly vulnerable. The survey on English housing carried out during 1997-8 recorded the sea of disorder to be around twice as high in inner cities and deprived areas of the country as a whole, let alone the richest areas. The results of this survey set a pattern of findings for all later enquiries on this issue. Moreover, it is probably this growing sense of disorder that has contributed to the greater fear of crime.

A very similar view was reported by landlords. They tallied, on average, 35 complaints a year from each 1,000 tenancies. A minority of landlords, in contrast, managing the most difficult areas, recorded a figure of up to 225 complaints for each 1,000 tenancies. One should not, however, simply conclude from this information that all poorer areas are equally affected by such behaviour. They are, generally speaking, most likely to be on the receiving end of such acts of viciousness. But pockets of very high anti-social behaviour in poorer areas exist cheek by jowl with other poorer areas where such behaviour is nowhere to be seen.

Complaints about anti-social behaviour are still an inaccurate gauge of what in reality is happening. Too many local residents know to their cost how ineffective complaints against the perpetuators of anti-social behaviour can be. Worse still, ineffective counter measures by landlords and the police can put the complainant at considerable risk.

The government report on unpopular housing referred to evidence of how, in some instances, a whole area can become decimated within a matter of months because of anti-social behaviour. In areas from which people were trying to escape, anti-social behaviour and crime head the list of reasons people gave for getting away.

In Birkenhead, to take a single example, a respectable area of terraced housing (comprising of 300 or so homes) was quickly decimated by the advent of just two dysfunctional families being moved into the area. The collapse was so quick and devastating that even an area which could boast a fair spread of owner-occupation now looks like Ramallah after a visit by the Israelis.

Once people began to move out of the area the streets quickly became littered with burned-out houses, security doors were ripped off from their posts, and metal window guards showed all the signs of being on the receiving end of battering rams. What was until very recently a decent working class area is now to be bulldozed at a total cost to taxpayers of £3-4m.

These one-off surveys on anti-social behaviour also recorded an increase in the time officials spent trying to counter such disorder. The report on unpopular housing, to which reference has already been made, recorded that fewer people felt safe than they did two years previously. This was reflected in the growing number of complaints recorded concerning anti-social behaviour. More and more police time is spent on disorder issues – up 19 per cent between 1995-96 and 1997-98.

Also over a two year period, beginning in 1996-97, local authorities reported a 127 per cent increase in the number of possession actions they had taken against anti-social tenants. During a slightly earlier period, 1993-97, the Chartered Institute of Environmental Health Officers recorded complaints about neighbours rising by 56 per cent. Likewise, reflecting on the past five years, 80 per cent of social landlords reported that legal action was used more frequently now than previously in cases of anti-social behaviour.

Poor people affected most

These snapshots capture, at a single point in time, the riders of the apocalypse – crime, disorder and anti-social behaviour. While the

British Crime Survey has asked questions about the extent of anti-social behaviour every two years commencing in 1992, in its latest survey, for 2000, much more detailed information was recorded. The results give us a moving picture highlighting the increase over time in anti-social behaviour.

The added value of how the BCS asked its questions about anti-social behaviour was that those criminal incidents, which respondents had mentioned in earlier questions in the survey, were excluded from the answers on anti-social behaviour. The results therefore excluded those acts of disorder which can be countered under the existing law, concentrating instead on such behaviour which results from the failure of individuals and families to practice decent behaviour which considered the needs of others. The findings from the survey were therefore nearer than other sources of information to anti-social behaviour as I have defined it, and on which I believe the political debate should concentrate.

About one in ten of the entire population reported that they had been on the receiving end of some form of anti-social behaviour during the last year. Young people being rude and abusive was reported by one in five of those experiencing anti-social behaviour. A further 15 per cent reported adults acting similarly, 12 per cent recorded disputes with their neighbours, 13 per cent local noise or disturbances, while drug related incidents resulted in anti-social behaviour for another 8 per cent.

Which groups are most affected by anti-social behaviour? On one count it looks very much as though it is the middle class, with 21 per cent of those reporting being insulted, pestered or intimidated during the previous year living in affluent urban areas. Further, 12 per cent reported separately on anti-social behaviour.

Affluent families reported 16 per cent and 11 per cent respectively as being affected by insulting or anti-social behaviour. In contrast, 16 per cent of residents on council estates registered instances where they were insulted or pestered or intimidated, with 9 per cent recording acts of anti-social behaviour against them.

Lurking behind these global figures however is another message. We know that fewer poor people work and that, generally speaking, poorer people travel less often, and less far than do more affluent groups. Quite properly the British Crime Survey recorded those instances of anti-social behaviour occurring at work, and while the person was in transit, as well as those acts locally based around the home.

Higher income groups were more likely to report being pestered, and experience other forms of anti-social behaviour while at work, or in the course of travelling. In contrast, the anti-social behaviour against the poor occurs around their own home, is carried out by local residents, and from which, as a consequence, it is more difficult, even impossible, for them to escape.

Once the rot starts

Winnie had lived in the street for over 40 years. Throwing human excrement over her wall was the final straw for her. She sought sheltered accommodation, and the opposite of what she had experienced over the previous twelve months.

It was following the move into the road, after eviction from another private sector house, that the anti-social behaviour swiftly changed gear for the worse. Had this eviction not taken place, neighbours, driven to despair and a failure of authorities to support them, threatened to beat the life out of the family.

The road consists of 100 houses. All but three of these families are decent working class people. With the arrival of one of the Adams boys who teamed up with one other lad of a similar age, they then joined forces with one of the children of a single mother, who left her children unattended as she worked to 2 to 3 am in the local bingo hall.

These three maladjusted boys are currently attacking one of the houses being renovated. They had previously whacked the occupant across the head with a board. After living in the road for 50 years he left. This house is now being renovated and the brick wall that had been rebuilt was pushed over by this little gang. A wooden defence wall has had to be built around the house.

No-one is safe to walk in the street. They are liable to be verbally attacked and children are not allowed out by themselves as they are likely to get smacked in the face. The language shouted at passers by is as foul as it is violently expressed.

'Appealing to the boys' mothers is like talking to a brick wall'. There are no father figures in these three families. Complaints to the authorities bring no respite.

This is partly because the families are in private accommodation and the landlords simply do not care how the tenants behave, providing their bank account registers the right amount of housing benefit on the right day. One landlord had been traced to London. His response was nothing if not simple. He had put people in power to sort these sorts of families out and, with that, he put down the phone.

The counter-stand has been lead by a father and son who show huge courage. Other families have cowered into silence. Yet this bravery is not inexhaustible.

'I am losing it' admits Terry. 'I have never been so often to one place as I have been to Manor Road (the local police station). But nothing happens. Officials don't give a toss how we live. These families have turned a decent place into a shit hole. I have been here 35 years. I have never seen anything like it. If we vote again it will be to vote out the councillors'.

A Wirral resident

Less chance of escape

The anti-social behaviour experienced by the poor is not only more locally based but much more likely to occur regularly rather than be experienced as a one off event while, for example, travelling. Equally significant, the commentary on the survey notes that those on low income were more likely to categorise their experience as problems associated with their neighbourhood.

It appears therefore that poorer people are more likely to categorise much anti-social behaviour as a 'local problem', which for the poor it certainly is, rather than name it as anti-social behaviour. In contrast richer people, who, when they experience anti-social behaviour, are more likely to do so away from their homes and were much more likely to record these experiences in a way which the surveyists immediately classified as anti-social behaviour.

Other findings likewise report clearly the link between being poor and being on the receiving end of anti-social behaviour as being more common and more likely to depress one's living standards. Indeed, the British Crime Survey gave a number of examples of just how much more significant anti-social behaviour was to poorer people. The returns showed, for example, 48 per cent of the unemployed, 44 per cent of students, 41 per cent of low income households and 50 per cent of those living in social housing recording anti-social type behaviour as having a negative impact on their quality of life.

Surprisingly, given the illustrations the media so often present of the issue, non-pensioners reported anti-social behaviour as a bigger issue affecting their lives than did pensioners. What is noticeable from the survey, however, is that people over 65 were much more likely than other groups to report disputes with neighbours, local noise or disturbances, and young people being rude, as constituting for them the bulk of anti-social behaviour.

Poor areas affected most

The British Crime Survey presented in its overall findings an individual's sense of disorder, and the extent to which this disorder devalued their quality of life. It presented this data in average terms for the whole country, as well as dividing the data into types of areas in which respondents lived. Six such sub-divisions were made and areas were ranked according to the proportion of people reporting a high sense of disorder in their area, which impacted on their quality of life.

Overall in England and Wales 14 per cent of people recorded a high sense of disorder, with 37 per cent experiencing disorder impacting adversely on their qualify of life. The group least affected by anti-social behaviour were affluent suburbs and affluent rural areas. Only 4 per cent of respondents in these areas reported a high sense of disorder.

At the other extreme came the replies from those living on council estates and other low income areas. Here 34 per cent of respondents reported a high sense of disorder and over half (54 per cent) saw anti-social behaviour reducing their quality of their life.

Within this poorest group, 51 per cent of those living on council estates in the greatest hardship recorded a high sense of disorder, and two-thirds saw anti-social behaviour undermining their quality of life. The equivalent figures for multi-ethnic and for low income areas were 54 per cent and 66 per cent respectively.

Conclusion

Crime, disorder and anti-social behaviour prosper most in particular areas. Where normal social control is weak, and where poverty is marked, the pattern of crime, disorder and anti-social behaviour becomes pronounced. In such areas, the riders of the apocalypse find life easy. It is not that one of these activities leads to another, it is rather that a certain environment gives rise to all three.

For working class communities, unlike areas dominated by the middle class, anti-social behaviour is very much locally induced and related. Moreover, the poor and working class families on whom anti-social behaviour is inflicted are less effective than middle class victims in using the law to counter such behaviour. A bank balance gives immediate access to lawyers and other professional services. If the law fails then the middle class have the option of simply moving away, an option other groups do not generally have. It is for this very reason that the demand for an effective strategy against anti-social behaviour is most strongly voiced in the poorest areas, for it is the good citizens who live nearest these dysfunctional families who suffer most.

So what is the solution? The size of the task cannot be over-estimated. No strategy has even a hope of success unless it galvanises society to the task. Central will be gaining a common answer to what kind of citizens its members should be. In beginning this process the past holds some key lessons on how big a project this is.

7. Turning the tide

Introduction

Anti-social behaviour is fast ploughing up what was Britain's peaceable kingdom. The causes of this fracturing are numerous. The clock cannot be turned back to recreate the forces which once shaped a common decency, as these are no longer practical politics. In place of the guidelines resulting from the interaction of evangelicalism and a growing civil society, Britain has to develop a contract-based citizenship to give a new form to the common decencies we inherited.

Taking Stock

Neighbours from Hell has defined anti-social behaviour more narrowly than it often is. There are a number of reasons for this. At the moment anti-social behaviour is all too often bracketed with general law and disorder issues and, like so much of that, all too often goes unchallenged. A necessary part of any counter-strategy is to separate that disorder, which could be dealt with under current legislation, and then to strike against these traditional forms of disorder as quickly as possible.

This approach will, of course, raise the crucial question of the size of the police budget and a reform of the legal system's procedures so that courts hear cases quickly. It is now easier to get a scarce NHS bed than it is to bring a criminal to justice.

A single anti-social behaviour act cannot be equated with, say, a mugging. It is the repetitious nature of these acts, day after day, night after night, which elevates anti-social behaviour into a major personal and political issue. Why do youths, and now some adults, behave in such an uncivilised manner?

The answer to this question is the key to understanding why *Neighbours from Hell* defines anti-social behaviour in the way it does. The root cause of anti-social behaviour stems from the failure of some families to promote a set of common decencies, which centre on a proper consideration of others. While a strategy is all too obviously necessary to check anti-social behaviour, it is also crucial simultaneously to tackle its root causes – the rise of dysfunctional families. Building up a much more responsive police and criminal justice system must go hand in hand with developing an effective counter-strategy that strikes at the foundations of anti-social behaviour.

Despite a recent increase in police budgets, there is no way that the current wave of lawlessness is going to be dealt with effectively by current policing levels. The cry 'it's anti-social behaviour' is now all too often a cover for the failure to deal with those forms of disorder that could be countered under the existing law, if resources were mobilised and the will to do so was there.

Of course the existing police resources need to be used as effectively as possible. The introduction of community support officers is welcome. Linking up with the fast burgeoning security industry, now employing more people than the combined totals of our police forces, makes good sense.

But, at the end of the day, a very significant increase in police resources is required if the current plague-like outbreak of lawlessness is to be countered. Throwing all kinds of disorder under the heading of anti-social behaviour may be a happy refuge for the muddled headed, but for politicians it is an all too easy diversion from a debate on the inadequacies of police staffing and resources.

The argument has been made that current legal provisions against lawlessness should be effectively enforced. This approach will require a greater police presence if it is to have any chance of success. Likewise, a revolutionary speeding-up in the timing of an offender's court appearance, and a decisive shift so that the law is weighted more towards those who have been offended against, is also required if current provisions are to stand a reasonable chance of countering lawlessness.

Similarly, the operation of the European Convention on Human Rights has to be radically rebalanced for the operation of the law to match much more closely the clear sense of fairness that most voters possess. But these changes alone will not turn back the tide of disorder.

A defining characteristic of anti-social behaviour not only comes from its newness, but from its root cause. And it is from a consideration of its cause that an indication is gained of how fundamental a change is occurring in what was once the natural ecology governing society. *Neighbours from Hell* has centred the cause of anti-social behaviour on the failure of families to teach their offspring those social virtues that balance a proper consideration for the needs of others with an individual's own wishes.

Lawlessness resulting from anti-social behaviour should not be viewed therefore as a temporary phenomena that will burn itself out. As an ever greater number of families become dysfunctional, an ever-increasing supply of socially offensive individuals results. *Neighbours from Hell* argues that anti-social behaviour poses a fundamental threat to a peaceable society. While new and more effective policing systems are required to hold the line against this semi-barbarism, the supply routes to anti-social behaviour must be simultaneously broken.

The second chapter of this book recorded how the behaviour of youths, freed from any sense of what constitutes common decencies, impacts on a neighbourhood's wellbeing. While it is true that most anti-social behaviour is committed by youths who are out of the control of their parents, or anyone else, its ugly face is now sometimes worn by whole families acting in a blind, irrational and, not to say, cruel way to their neighbours.

Not surprisingly therefore, but most worryingly for the longer-term, anti-social behaviour is beginning to wear an ever younger face. More children are now excluded from Birkenhead junior schools because of their behaviour than their secondary school counterparts.

Perpetual uncertainty

Totalitarian regimes know that human beings need a high degree of certainty if they are to live happy and free lives. Such regimes therefore organise themselves to deny such certainty, knowing that its absence makes it that much easier to control and subject the populace. An individual, family or neighbourhood inflicted with anti-social behaviour is similarly stripped of the certainty that is crucial for happiness and wellbeing.

Anti-social behaviour snatches away that certainty an individual needs to live out their life without the fear of being on the receiving end of endless annoyance, which sometimes becomes so frequent it is little short of terror. The certainty of going about one's normal business without fear is ruptured.

One's home is no longer one's castle. It is invaded by anti-social behaviour from, as we saw, surprise attacks on windows, jumping on roofs and even fouling through letterboxes. Sleep is no longer guaranteed.

Schools are no longer no go zones for such gross behaviour. Indeed, it is here that we can plot most easily how the balance of forces in this battle for decent behaviour is moving. The natural authority that society requires for its proper functioning is being overrun by the storm troopers of nihilistic behaviour.

And, as this group asserts the paramountcy of its view over everyone else's, the role of natural authority that accompanies both office and age is destroyed. It is becoming ever more necessary for that authority, which is fundamental to the operation of a free society, and which was once freely accepted, to be imposed.

The diminishing role of natural authority marches hand in hand with the devaluing of truth and, equally importantly, a growing unwillingness to stand up and be counted in its defence. This growing defencelessness of truth is apparent in what would have, at one time, seemed the relatively safe confines of the school.

In schools the tide of opinion has subtly shifted. Outside the shift is more noticeable. Fewer and fewer people below retirement age are willing, for example, to testify in court against their tormentors.

This summary of how anti-social behaviour not only impacts, but how the roots of this behaviour are being nurtured, should disillusion anyone who believes there is a panacea out there waiting to be discovered. Countering anti-social behaviour isn't a task for the feint hearted.

Our peaceable kingdom, which is now being ploughed up by anti-social behaviour, did not fall into place by accident. That is the important lesson of chapter three of this book.

The kind of society Britain became, a century or more ago, was the result of the determined effort of a growing majority of its citizens. A public ideology was hammered out, lived and supported by the population as a whole. An unwritten citizenship contract reigned.

We are the inheritors of social capital that provided the building blocks for this society. The sources of this capital are not now available. Christianity, while important, is no longer in the possession of the writ it once held. But that simple evangelical creed, centering on how each of us should use our lives, needs recreating by secular means.

Welfare has been largely nationalised and its self-imposed discipline lost. These changes have left cruelly exposed the band of society's initiators of the young. How can they guide behaviour when the forces arguing that everything is relative hold the field?

The task is one upon which the whole of society has to be engaged. But how can general statements on rebuilding a shared sense of common decencies be achieved? Merely repeating the phrase will all too quickly become vacuous.

To ward off this fate, the exercise has to be grounded in the practical aspects of daily living. And the best way of doing this is to begin forging a series of contracts which cover the behaviour of all of us as we negotiate the public realm.

How can the idea of the duties of citizenship be entrenched in a whole series of contracts so that each begins to reinforce each other, building up thereby into an overarching political contract? These contracts need to cater for each key stage in our life, at birth, at school, in work, in drawing welfare and at retirement.

If the tide is to be turned, and anti-social behaviour put to flight, the task is nothing less than the forging of a series of public contracts on behaviour, tightly drawn at first, so agreement can be quickly obtained. If they are going to help shape behaviour these contracts have to be built up, taught and enforced.

What might constitute each of these contracts? How can they be best taught? How can they be defended? Answers to these questions form the subject matter of the remaining chapters.

Conclusion

It is not only in its newness that anti-social behaviour poses such a threat to society. More fundamental, and more worrying, is its root cause. Without tackling the root cause of anti-social behaviour – the rise of dysfunctional families who fail to teach their offspring common decencies – Britain can expect an ever-rising tide of lawlessness.

Turning the tide against the new nihilists will require a much more effective holding operation by the police. But it also requires simultaneously the development of contract politics aimed at the root cause of anti-social behaviour. New strategies for policing, welfare and education are required.

8. The police as surrogate parent

Introduction

Neighbours from Hell has sketched out my belief that anti-social behaviour's recruiting sergeant is the dysfunctional family. Those families who fail to teach their young a proper respect for others invariably have little idea how to control the resulting breakdown in normal behaviour. Helping families succeed requires a long-term strategy and this is considered in Chapter ten. An immediate need is for substitute or surrogate parents to step in to the breach. The only body which can immediately hold the line in this way is the police.

Youth annoyance

As politics changed I tried quite early on to use what my constituents were telling me as the ammunition with which to change policy. What new weapons against anti-social behaviour could be more effectively fashioned? At first, much of the information relayed to me by aggrieved constituents centred on the behaviour of gangs of boys, some aged as young as six.

Their behaviour, which made life so impossible for those affected, ranged, as I recalled in chapter two, from such acts as urinating and defecating through letterboxes, trampling over flower beds, smashing garden fences, swearing at adults, particularly pensioners, and damaging to the point of destruction garages by clambering on to them and letting rip. More recently, a small but significant number of adolescent girls have joined their male counterparts in unruly and uncouth behaviour.

The amount of police time dedicated to attempting to counter anti-social behaviour has risen sharply. As early as the mid 1990s, the police in Birkenhead estimated that around 40 to 50 per cent of their time was spent dealing with such instances of youth annoyance.

The phrase 'youth annoyance' was employed as a collective term for a whole series of offences. One single offence was not deemed serious enough to warrant a formal caution. It was the cumulative impact of each of these aggressive acts which had a destroying effect on people's lives equal to that of the more serious acts.

The 1994 Criminal Justice Act extended the scope of the Children's and Young Persons' Act of 1933 by allowing a court to make an order against a child convicted of an offence for which adults can be punished with 14 years' imprisonment, plus indecent assault of a woman and causing death by dangerous driving. Welcome as these powers were in dealing with some of the most frightening of criminal acts by young people, the 1994 changes did nothing to begin building an effective strategy against youth disorder and annoyance.

Locally based reform programme

In 1996, the Labour Party was beginning to formulate its own policy against anti-social behaviour and it invited interested parties to say how they saw the issue and, on the basis of this, propose what might be done. The resulting paper entitled *Tackling Youth Crime: Reforming Youth Justice* threw out a challenge as to how we might reform the justice system to make juveniles responsible for their actions and, in the process, deter others from the kind of behaviour that was becoming so damaging to the local community.

In a submission to the Party on how best to develop its counter anti-social behaviour strategy, I put forward four suggested reforms. By far the most important centred on how best immediately to counter unacceptable behaviour. Each of the suggested changes were based on how the current law and procedure failed to deal effectively with anti-social behaviour in Birkenhead.

The first suggested reform centred on the immediate issue with which my constituents had confronted me. How could the semi-barbarous acts of children and young people be better controlled? The idea I put forward was for a cautions-type system against youth annoyance, or, as it became known, anti-social behaviour. The proposal was based on the system of cautions which operate on football pitches which may end with a red card, sending off the offending player. A new formal youth annoyance caution was the suggested reform.

What constitutes annoyance is clearly a matter of judgement. One group which is well placed to judge this is the group on the receiving end of this anti-social behaviour. But while this group knows only too well what anti-social behaviour is, it cannot, for obvious reasons, be the body which levies the penalty points.

A youth or magistrates court, on the other hand, would fulfil the conditions of separating the adjudicating function on whether penalty points should be applied. The downside to giving courts the duty to adjudicate is their notorious slowness in administering justice, so much so that a question mark is raised over whether justice, which is so long delayed, is justice at all.

Which body could adjudicate effectively, quickly, but who would also be regarded by most people as operating fairly? The proposal was for youth annoyance cautions to be issued on the spot by policemen and policewomen, providing the incident fitted what was generally agreed to be youth annoyance.

An individual youth could be cautioned. Any youth who was seen as part of a wider group committing annoyance would also be liable to be cautioned, while whole groups of youths could similarly be cautioned for causing such annoyance. The proposal also envisaged the possibility of three penalty points being issued for a single offence if it was serious enough.

This proposed reform was that if a young person kept repeatedly committing youth annoyance offences, and if he or she accumulated a designated number of such offences, a suggestion of three was made, the offender would be punished by restrictions being placed on what they could do and where they could go.

The assumption underpinning a penalty points system was made explicit. An immediate reason why so many young people were behaving in an aggressively annoying fashion to some of their neighbours was, as often as not, due to the parents' failure to control their offspring's behaviour. This failure was sometimes due to a parental lack of interest, sometimes due to an inability to do much about their offspring's behaviour, although the wish to act was there.

I believe that a new police role could be developed if the authority parents should exercise in enforcing good behaviour in their young was transferred, where necessary, to individual policemen and women. Under a penalty points system the police could become a substitute parental figure for those parents who cannot or will not control their children.

What would constitute annoyance? It would not be concerned, for example, with actions of young people to whom a busybody neighbour had taken exception. Little groups of complainants can be effectively organised to a degree that their organisational strength does not reflect the objectivity of their case.

Many police have a good nose for what is really happening. Besides, their judgement would be open to appeal, and this fact itself would enter into the policeman or women's approach to judging whether the action warranted a caution.

Indeed, the major check against abuse of this new power would be an appeal to a youth or magistrates court. The police would have the power to propose a penalty system which would lead to restrictions being placed on the offender. These restrictions would operate immediately until a court had overthrown the original decision.

In this way, the current slowness of court hearings would be sidestepped. Respite for the community under attack would be secured. An appearance before fellow citizens on the bench would be guaranteed. But it would be in the form of an appeal against the surrogate parent's decision.

The surrogate parent's power would not be negated until the courts had decided that that was the right course of action.

Moreover, the surrogate parent would not only have the power to restrict activities. As importantly, the police should have the power to compel offending young people to undertake positive tasks in the community, which would hopefully build up a more constructive attitude to the community.

The rise of ASBOs

In place of the suggested youth annoyance caution schemes, the newly elected Labour government brought forward anti-social behaviour orders or, as they quickly became known, ASBOs. Confidence that the new system would work easily and smoothly led the government to claim that 5000 orders would be issued each year once the 1998 Crime and Disorder Bill became law.

That was the plan. In practice, ASBOs turned out to be not only difficult to register but immensely time-consuming to secure. Instead of 15,000 orders expected to be made during the first three years after the Act came into force, less than 500 orders were granted.

At the end of 2002, not one had been issued covering the Birkenhead area despite attempts at a co-ordinated drive by the police. The first attempt to obtain such an order, which ate up something like 400 hours of local agencies' time, ended in failure.

This local experience was used to lobby the then incoming Home Secretary, David Blunkett, to simplify radically the procedures for gaining such orders. In no way did the original ASBOs meet the urgency which constituents believed the circumstances demanded.

It was unlikely that the government would admit to bad judgment in going down the ASBO route, rather than the much simpler proposal of a penalty points system. Yet spending 400 hours and failing to gain an ASBO was as deeply demoralising for staff as it was unsatisfactory for the citizens seeking adequate protection from the new barbarism.

I therefore proposed to the government that they simplify the procedure so that the culprits could make an early entry into court; restrictions on the offender's freedom could be imposed, together with, hopefully, constructive proposals on how they might spend their time.

A strict timetable would simultaneously be agreed with the court, stating when the authorities would need to return with fuller evidence as well as setting a time limit for the ASBO's life. This simplified ASBO procedure was legislated for under the Criminal Justice and Police Act 2001. The first such order was gained for Birkenhead in February 2003.

Still too slow

Two issues arise from this welcome modification of ASBOs. The first centres on the limited speed by which interim orders are gained. While the detailed work necessary for a full ASBO is temporarily side-stepped, a range of detailed work still has to be undertaken for the initial court hearing.

This work is, of course, not lost for it forms the basis of the submission for a full ASBO. But an interim order not only requires a substantial amount of work over a longish period of time, it is also dependent on a slot being quickly found in a court's timetable so that an application can be made.

The second issue about interim and full ASBOs is whether they are a too cumbersome and time-consuming approach for what is required in the first instance. Again, there is an assumption here about how anti-social behaviour takes off in the local community. Not only is there a need for rules, but there is an immediate requirement for authority to act when they are defied.

Disorder quickly feeds disorder. It spreads like the plague as more and more young people are sucked into disorder who would not otherwise have so acted. They become part of a disorderly gang because no-one has the authority and power immediately to check unacceptable behaviour.

Worse then follows. Part of the gang goes on quickly to commit acts that are way beyond anyone's definition of anti-social behaviour. A certain madness grows within the group's behaviour.

What is most necessary, and still so singularly lacking, is the quickest of checks on bad behaviour when it first displays itself. Even with interim ASBOs we still do not have the rapid response necessary to block effectively the spread of unacceptable behaviour.

The failure to be able to so act ends in misery for the community and, ultimately, equal misery for the offender. Jason, whose behaviour featured in chapter two, went unchecked for years, is now in prison and has thereby gained a criminal record, but not before his character had spun out of any resemblance with normality. His major drinking problem is ignored and there is precious little support to help him confront the other reasons why he is in such a wretched state.

The first part of a new strategy to counter anti-social behaviour must be the introduction of surrogate parents. The only viable body who can play such a role equally throughout the country is the police.

But again, the question of resources pushes its ugly head back high up on the agenda. New functions will require more policemen and women. And even if this function is given to the new community support officers, and I think allowing this group of officers also the power of awarding penalty points would enhance their status and authority in the community, a larger police budget would be necessary. How this might be gained is considered in chapter eleven.

Further reforms

The introduction of surrogate parenthood was the first suggestion made to the Labour Party back in 1996. Three other reforms were also made as part of a more comprehensive reform package.

A second suggested reform dealt with the age at which children could be held responsible for their actions. The law then defined responsibility by age. On the basis of what I had learned from my constituents I believed the law should be changed so that by merely committing certain designated acts, a person was deemed old enough to be held accountable for those actions. This was a proposal which was supported by a number of other bodies lobbying the Labour Party at the time and was seen into law as part of the Crime and Disorder Act 1998. Progress on the other two suggested reforms is still lacking.

A third proposed reform centred on Secure Training Orders. These orders were introduced in 1994 and applied only to young people. Again, on the basis of what I had been taught locally, I saw the need to drop the age restriction which applied to these.

As a fourth reform, and linked to making the issue of secure training orders effective, I argued for a significant increase in the number of secure places to which offenders could be sent. By February 2003, there were still less than 3000 places throughout the whole country.

This last reform was based on a second assumption which underpins this group of reforms. If society was to use deterrents to change behaviour, those deterrents had to be delivered. It was no use sanctioning by way of a secure training order if a place at a secure training centre, or similar body, was not available for all those so sentenced by a youth court. That sanction is still inadequate and prevents all the serious ring leaders being taken out of circulation quickly and effectively.

Community Prosecution Laywers

A further reform is necessary. Crime impacts most severely on poorer people and is most pronounced in the poorest areas. Anti-social behaviour reflects this pattern. The position of those on the sharp end of such behaviour needs to be directly strengthened.

A very modest reform would be to ensure that those citizens who are prepared to testify against the thug have a separate court waiting room. At the moment too many witnesses have to sit facing their tormentors while awaiting the start of the trial. All sorts of threats, real or imagined, take place here and a knowledge that, after enduring anti-social behaviour over a long period of time, the innocent are subjected to yet another round of harassment, must act as an all too powerful deterrent to appearing in court.

More radical reform is required to strengthen the position of the citizen against the new nihilists. The current policy of operating against the most serious crimes must of course continue. But part of the Crown Prosecution Service's (CPS) budget should be spent on what local people believe to be the main priorities inviting disorder.

The CPS should be overhauled so that it has an appropriate number of staff operating on a constituency basis. Currently the mode of operation is regional. The head of each of these offices should become an elected post and this person would, in the first instance, be concerned with enforcing all anti-social behaviour legislation. The election of these community prosecution lawyers would ensure that local prosecution policies reflect local demands, or the office holder would find themselves quickly without a job.

Conclusion

Anti-social behaviour in large part arises from dysfunctional families failing to teach their children common standards of decency centring on respect for other people. Helping families succeed has to be part of an overall strategy, which restores a greater sense of order and common decency to our society. At the same time, parents in difficulties with their children, some of whose behaviour is as bad as their children, need to be supported by surrogate parents.

The surrogate parents need to be given by society an authority to check bad behaviour and, as with good natural parents, the surrogates need the power to restrict an offending youth's behaviour immediately without going to court. Electing community prosecution lawyers would ensure that the CPS prosecution policy reflects more readily the wish for a much more effective policy of sanctions against crime in general, and the rise of the yobbish culture in particular. The dividing line between acceptable and unacceptable behaviour would thereby be quickly reinforced. Such guidance needs to be applied more generally and we now turn to how welfare can also act in this teaching role.

9. Welfare as teacher

Introduction

The idea that welfare should be received free of conditions is a very recent development. For most of the past four hundred years the receipt of welfare has been dependent on fulfilling a series of conditions. Only since the 1960s did an opposing idea gain ground until it was held to be the only proper view. Welfare now needs to fulfil its two traditional roles of providing income while simultaneously giving clear guidance as to what is acceptable and unacceptable behaviour.

Welfare and abundance

Confidence was high. Economic growth would provide such abundance that the age old political agenda – who gets what, when and how – would soon pass forever into the history books. The new politics would centre on how to distribute abundance. Likewise, the curing power of socialism would dispense the curse of Adam. This perfectibility of mankind could be achieved by human means. These were the hidden assumptions underpinning the sweet dawn philosophy by which progressive forces graced the 1960s.

We now know better. Economic growth proved illusory. The economy went on determinedly in much the same old way, spluttering out bursts of fast growth followed by equally sharp reversals. And the gentlest lunacy about the perfectibility of human nature, the yardstick by which left wing status was awarded, opened up the 1980s and most of the 1990s to Mrs Thatcher and her cohorts.

One aspect of the 1960s heritage still rolls around the heads of those on the centre-left, causing much confusion. In the age of abundance the idea that welfare should be provided conditional on the claimant's behaviour seemed to be a throwback to wicked Victorian times.

The new conventional wisdom viewed benefits being provided simply because people needed them, or on the grounds that they paid the requisite insurance contributions. To require claimants to jump through further qualifying hoops before gaining benefit might have been appropriate in an age of scarcity. But not in this new dawn.

Although the idea that benefits should be delivered unconditionally mesmerised much of the political elite, most voters were sceptical about this aspect of the new age. Behavioural conditions have traditionally been attached to drawing benefit. And voters seethe with a degree of righteousness as they witness some of the people, whose welfare is paid for by their taxes, behave in a way that makes normal life for them impossible.

Conditionality

The first move to re-establish conditions being attached to benefit was made in 1986 when the then Conservative government required all claimants unemployed for six months or more to attend what were called Restart Interviews. Claimants could also be required to join Jobclubs where they could more actively look for work.

The Left dismissed these moves as offering no help to the unemployed. Their real aims, we were assured, were to rough up those without work, while at one and the same time persuading the public that many of those standing in the dole queues were responsible for their own idleness. It is true that these measures were based on an assumption that some of the unemployed were working on the side and that Restart and Jobclubs would make this fraud a little more difficult to perpetuate. But the new conditions attached to drawing benefit were also ones that help individuals make the most of matching their abilities to job opportunities.

Welfare and behaviour

Attaching specific behaviour conditions to benefit signals a fundamental change in welfare's role. The case for this move therefore needs to be spelt out. Also the extent to which such a reform is a legitimate extension of the now work related conditions to drawing benefit needs similar explanation.

I supported the Conservative government strategy of adding conditions that had to be fulfilled if long-term claimants were to continue to draw benefit. My reasons for doing so were different from those put forward by the government. The assumptions I held for supporting work related conditions being attached to drawing benefit are similar to those underpinning extending conditionality to behaviour.

Economists at that time were arguing that the severity of unemployment in the 1980s had resulted in the market being so weakened that it no longer had any inbuilt stimulus to move back to full employment. An economic hysteresis had occurred.

I witnessed in my constituency a social hysteresis whereby prolonged unemployment broke up those traditional patterns of behaviour amongst some of the unemployed which normally led to individuals seeking jobs at the earliest opportunity. Prolonged unemployment broke the spirit of many of the unemployed, and the sight of such people was a wretched spectacle. A terrible fatalism that 'I will never work again' descended upon whole tranches of individuals in areas of record joblessness.

Proactive welfare was for me essentially about repairing the local social ecology so that the norm and expectation would once again be that wherever possible people worked instead of drawing welfare. The new conditions attached to drawing benefits – Restart interviews and membership of Jobclubs – were about trying to help re-engender the work ethic. A similar exercise is now required to repair the social ecology that feeds a common decency culture. At every opportunity society's institutions need to speak out clearly in support of behaviour which gives a proper place to the needs of others.

Making acceptable behaviour a new condition for drawing welfare has to be part of a much wider strategy. But crucial to any success on this front is the removal of the so damaging belief that no matter how badly a person behaves their right to welfare is inviolate. The link has to be broken whereby continual offensive behaviour leaves that individual's right to benefit untouched.

Welfare and acceptable behaviour

For the majority of the population the establishment of a raft of rights to welfare has been wholly beneficial, freeing them from the fear of destitution. This impact has not, however, been universal. Taking out this supportive assumption that welfare will always be paid irrespective of a claimant's behaviour, is a crucial part of any successful strategy to re-establish common decencies.

But making welfare conditional on acceptable behaviour will run into the same kind of opposition that greeted the bill to withdraw housing benefit from neighbours from hell. So, once again, the premise upon which this strategy is based needs to be spelt out as clearly as possible.

The aim is not to score as many hits as possible. It would be marvellous if it were possible to change the whole climate of behaviour without applying any sanctions. But life is not sadly lived out for the most part in such storybook conditions. So while some scalps will have to be claimed, the change being wrought should be seen as part of enforcing a wider agenda; the establishment of a new understanding of the basis of citizenship.

Introducing specific welfare contracts is not an act which will single welfare out for different treatment. To the extent that there is different treatment is because there is at the moment no welfare contract. In an age of contracts welfare is distinguished by the absence of a formal binding contract between the individual on the one hand, and society on the other.

Building a formal contract here will align welfare with most other areas of life. In the age of consumerism the contract rules. The development of a formal welfare contract should within a fairly short time sit happily with the other contracts to which we sign up.

Houses are bought on mortgage contracts. Tenants have to sign tenancy agreements. There is a written and unwritten contract, for example, for each of us while we are at work. Employees have to turn up to work on time, perform their duties, often dress in a certain way and behave with a degree of civility to their colleagues. Pay and continual employment is conditional on meeting these basic but fundamental requirements.

Welfare contract

The welfare contract, which would be the beginnings of a codification of the responsibilities of the state and the individual to each other, should be in two parts, each one setting out what is expected of both parties to the agreement. On the government side, the contract should detail the contribution and income qualifying rules, together with the rights to benefit in a form which can be legally enforced by the claimant. The right to receive an annual statement on the contributions made and the benefit entitlement earned would form a cornerstone of society's side to the welfare contract. Included also would be the service that claimants would have a right to expect in the delivery of their benefits.

How to register for benefit, the time periods for responding to such requests, the right to privacy when pursuing a claim, the right to courteous treatment, the right to deal with an alternative member of staff, as well as the right to appeal against a decision, would also form part of society's side of the bargain.

The contract should be presented as a two sided document. The aim must be for each citizen to see that duties and rights are two sides of the same coin. When examining duties each of us will be able to turn over the contract and see what rights follow from fulfilling these duties. Similarly, those of us who begin reading the contract listing our rights, will, when turning over, see that each of these rights backs on, and is dependent upon the carrying out of a similar range of duties.

The rights provided by the community, and detailed in the first part of the contract, should now be backed by the duties each citizen will be expected to fulfil. The new citizen contract would also spell out for the first time the duties society places on citizens by linking them to benefit entitlements.

The duties side of the document would include the kind of citizens we as society wish each of us to be. The cardinal virtues of citizenship would be listed. And these virtues would be grounded in a general statement of how citizens will be expected to behave towards each other in order not to cause a continual grievance or annoyance. The consequences of a failure to maintain this standard of behaviour will be spelt out.

Being a good citizen, of putting more into society than one takes out, has long been part of the unwritten contract which most citizens have operated as part of the natural order. The vast majority of people will view the individual's side of the contract as codifying what they had previously taken for granted.

Yet its existence will play an important supporting role, adding certainty to the beliefs of the majority of the population who continue to prize civilised behaviour. The contract will signal for those citizens that, far from standing alone, society stands shoulder to shoulder with them, is signed up to their values and their views of the world which these values express.

The contract will therefore have an important role in strengthening the position of those whose position as teacher, social worker, youth leader or voluntary worker requires the upholding of these basic values of citizenship. For too long these key activists in civil society have felt isolated in their attempt to teach younger people what is expected of them. By making official what the ground rules of basic behaviour are, the position of those in authority who are expected to teach, as well as those who enforce such rules, will be immeasurably strengthened.

Rolling out the programme

The politics of introducing contract-based citizenship are considered in chapter eleven. Here it is assumed that the political process of introducing the idea, and seeing it through to legislation, would be successfully negotiated. How then would the welfare contract be rolled out? Where might such a reform start?

The registration of a birth offers a suitable starting point for rolling-out the programme. A new initiation, or welcoming ceremony, linked together with the gateway to claiming child benefit on a permanent basis, and the whole range of help and support for children and parents, would be brought together.

When the British expeditionary force sailed to France on the eve of World War One, practically every soldier had been baptised. Now, less than a century later, only 35 per cent of all children are given their name by baptism and formally welcomed into a wider community which extends beyond the immediate family. A new civil ceremony should now take on the near universal role that baptism once performed.

For this to be achieved the registration of a birth should cease to be a hurried, private affair between a parent and a state official. The registration of births should become the initiation ceremony to the wider society beyond an individual family and, in terms of society's duties to provide support, the registration should be the gateway to child benefit. Accompanying this right to benefit, the contract should detail the rights parents have in respect to post-natal and other NHS care, as well as access to Sure Start, nursery and school facilities [see panel on the page 105].

Parental duties would be stated in terms of how they can best make use of these facilities so as to give their child the very best possible start in life. The contract would succinctly detail why post-natal care, Sure Start, play group and nursery education are the rights the community has given to their child, and why it so important for parents to access these facilities on behalf of their child. In addition, the values the community both prizes and expects from its citizens would command a key passage in this citizenship registration.

The details on the contract will necessarily be brief. But each item on the duties parents have and the duties society has to help parents succeed, will be on the basis of the national curriculum's parenting classes (This proposal is picked up in the following chapter). The theme will also be part of the refresher classes couples have as they approach parenthood for the first time.

Signing the contract at the registration of the birth would also offer again parenting courses aimed at first-time parents and which would centre on the basis for a healthy and happy child. What the advent of a child is likely to mean to the relationship between parents should also be part of the package.

Every new parent I have asked has been enthusiastic about being offered such an opportunity, explaining how the huge new responsibilities they have gained are in no way matched by sympathetic support. Many new parents describe the near terror they feel when their baby is brought home, the various parties withdraw, the front door closes and they are on their own for the very first time.

The attractiveness of these courses would be enhanced if there had been a sustained public campaign on their importance and value. And, for the group who would gain most from the courses, their attractiveness would be yet further advanced if someone with appea,l like David Beckham, headed the campaign on why he and Posh are amongst the key promoters.

Beckham's involvement would be electric amongst the target audience of young males. As a cult figure for young people he is out on his own. The natural way he holds his children, takes them about, makes a priority of returning from trips as soon as possible to be with them, sends out an unambiguous message on what being a good dad involves.

The whole ethos would be that these are courses for every parent. An enthusiastic take-up would prevent such a move being seen as laying on courses only for failed or inadequate parents.

The registration of a birth would become an important ceremony in its own right. The registering of a new citizen would occur and would be celebrated by the community with the clear declaration of the duties the community has to each child and the duties each parent has to the child.

Registering the birth of a child at a local registry office would be one option, with an appropriate civil ceremony. Churches should be given the opportunity to add the citizenship rights of welcoming a child into our society to run alongside a baptismal service which welcomes the child into the wider church community. The government may later wish to see if the other bodies of civil society, the trade unions, and the local school, for example, would like to become organisations through which the initiation of citizenship can take place.

Child, Parent and Society's Contract

Your child has a right

1. To be brought up in a safe, secure and stimulating environment.
2. To have close and affectionate loving relationships, especially with you as parents.
3. To have high standards of care and good examples of behaviour.
4. To have an appropriate education.
5. To be protected against abuse.
6. To be guided and supported in the move towards independence and adulthood.

In order to help you as parents carry out your duties as parents, society lays down for you certain rights. The main rights cover

1. The provision of pre and post conception care and the universally provided free health care.
2. A minimum income together with child benefit.
3. Advice on the best practice for nurturing and securing the best future for your child.
4. Access to free education, the right to choose the school for your child, information about the progress of your child at school, appeals against decisions on which you are unhappy, details of how the parent school groups, as well as schools themselves are run.
5. Access to your child, and the ability to enjoy the company of your child, for parents not living with their child.

Each of these rights and duties would then be more fully explained

Rolling out other contracts

Linking a contract to the registration of a birth is one to be achieved over a life time, but it would commence with all births after a set date. Rolling out contracts for other benefits would operate in a similar fashion. They would commence at a set date for all individuals and families as they register for other benefits: income support, jobseekers' allowance, incapacity benefit and housing benefit, for example.

At each point, when an individual registers for benefit, part of the application would be to sign up to the citizenship contract which would be explained to them by the officer who is helping them register for benefit. Rolling out contracts, linking housing benefit to decent behaviour, should be an early candidate for action. While much anti-social behaviour is carried out by children and youths, often out of control of their parents, there is now a new breed of whole families, dubbed 'neighbours from hell', who systematically terrorise their neighbours.

The government's current plans for universalising model tenancy contracts for social housing tenants should be extended to tenants of private landlords. Likewise, these contracts should be linked to housing benefit sanctions for those families who fail to behave decently. Again, the theme will be a tenancy contract setting out people's rights while similarly emphasising that the exercise of these rights is dependent on duties.

The programme for the registration of people reaching eligibility for the state retirement pension would also commence, but this regime would be given a totally different emphasis. Here the community would take the opportunity of thanking the individual for completing successfully a working life, whether paid or unpaid and, as well as ensuring that payments for the state retirement pension were in place, information on opportunities open to people in the third and fourth age would be given.

While one side of the new pension contract would detail the values which pensioners would continue to subscribe to, the contract would also detail rights to income and health care. The opportunity of issuing this contract to those of retirement age should be used to signal a determined push against the ageism which is a marked feature in employment and some aspects of health care.

The celebration and registration of the birth of a citizen, the signing of pupils' school contracts (explained in the next chapter), the contracts for drawing income support, housing benefit, incapacity benefit and the like, and the celebratory contract for citizens as they reach the state retirement age, will each offer the community the opportunity to teach through the registrar, priest, teacher, trade union official or benefit clerk, what the duties and rights of citizenship involve. For most citizens, what is required of them will be par for the course. How citizenship is much more actively taught and, hopefully, embraced will be discussed in the next chapter.

Enforcing the new contract

To be effective, contracts have to be enforced. There has been some comment from government sources that they would see teachers amongst others enforcing fines on parents who fail, for example, to fulfil the minimum requirements of parenthood. I hope the government will think twice about such an enforcement strategy.

There clearly needs to be some threshold which, when crossed, triggers some action, with such triggering being decided by the health visitor, teacher or benefit clerk. But the function of deciding that a line has been crossed should be kept totally separate from deciding that a particular sanction should now be imposed. The agency deciding what action should follow a repeated failure to meet a contract should be the police, and only the police.

The aim is to maximise the agreement and the self-policing of these new contracts. But there will be examples where an enforcement procedure is required and, in this small minority of cases, the enforcement will be against children and/or their parents only after a careful warning of what will happen unless the behaviour of the individual or family changes swiftly for the better.

Once the police have the requisite evidence to levy a sanction, and then lodge that decision, the sanction should automatically come into operation on the appropriate benefit. Individuals would have a right to appeal to a youth, a family or magistrates court if they wished to contest the penalty.

It is crucial that the reasons for the penalties are explained and how specifically the penalties relate to how that individual has broken one or more aspects of their citizenship contract. Part of this procedure should be to explain the rights of appeal the individual has to an appropriate youth or family court. But the penalties would apply unless a court overturned them.

Applying sanctions will not only offer a further opportunity to explain why our society is intent on gaining agreement to its citizenship contracts. Applying a sanction should also give the opportunity for society to offer yet further help to the person who is breaking their contract in one or more respects.

For parents, whose children are genuinely out of control, an action programme would be agreed on how best to bring them back into control. Similarly, the long-term disadvantages that follow from not ensuring as effective post-natal care as possible will again be explained to a mother of a young child who has failed to bring the child to the clinic.

It is worth stressing again that the aim of any system of sanctioning is to change behaviour, not mindlessly to apply the sanctions. Explaining the nature of the tenancy agreement, for example, is important. So too is the existence of an arbitration system for neighbour disputes. Likewise, the intensive work with the most disruptive families, such as the one carried out in Dundee, has a part to play. But so too does a system of sanctions for those who, after all the support being offered, wilfully set about destroying the peace of the neighbourhood in which they live.

Conclusion

The view that welfare should be offered without strings attached is very much a product of the 1960s. For most of the last four hundred years, conditions have always been attached to drawing welfare payments. Conditionality was reintroduced in the 1980s to help the long-term unemployed find jobs when such jobs became available. Making welfare dependant on good behaviour should be part of a new citizenship contract. Contracts govern many areas of life and the new welfare contracts would bring welfare in from the cold. The understanding of these contracts needs to be enhanced through our education system. How that objective might be achieved is the topic to which we now turn.

10. Education as parent

Introduction

Religion was the most important driving force in Victorian society in teaching people the basis of the good life, and thereby what citizenship entailed. That option is not now open to us. Where once evangelicals were the great teaching force, schools must step into the breach. Surveys show that young people, in particular, now see citizenship in terms of good character, and believe that such character should be fostered within schools. Why and how schools are to achieve this objective will be a key part of establishing the politics of behaviour.

Note of hope

Despite the despair recorded on so many of these pages, significant developments are afoot. A clear sign of a second spring comes from a national survey contrasting the attitudes on citizenship of 15-24 year olds with the beliefs held by older generations. Given the concern there is over the behaviour of some young people, readers could be forgiven in bracing themselves for yet another blast of pessimism. The reverse is true. Of particular importance is the significant change in what this younger group judge as to what makes for a good citizen.

While young people feel less attached to the local community, and do not feel quite the same pull towards their country as do their parents and grandparents, they nevertheless have an intriguing view about citizenship. For them, the meaning of citizenship is not writ in simple terms of rights and duties. And when it is expressed in these terms, younger people emphasise duties more than they highlight rights.

Citizenship is defined by this younger group in terms of character rather than community. For young people respect for others is the most valued characteristic of good citizenship. The next desirable characteristic is to be law abiding and to have respect for the environment. The third characteristic of good citizenship is setting a good example to others. It is hard to think of better results for any society serious about rebuilding a peaceable and contented kingdom.

There is also widespread agreement that schools should teach citizenship. Practically the whole of the sample thought so. But the views of younger people, that citizenship should centre on the kind of person each of us should be, give a distinctive approach to the programme which they wish to see taught in schools.

The difference between young and old of course should not be overemphasised for the survey shows a large degree of overlap. It is, however, the emphasis younger respondents gave to developing good character that holds a great potential for reshaping the school syllabus.

According to the report's authors, 'Good character is in'. Younger people wish to see good citizenship taught around the ideas of having respect for others, as well as for the environment. Teaching of values is in, while the descriptive teaching of civic institutions is relegated to the sidelines.

Remaking citizenship

Remaking a strong sense of citizenship requires a careful and sustained campaign. Such a campaign poses questions as to what kind of political strategy is most likely to gain success on this front, and that very question is taken up in the following chapter.

The objective of the political strategy is clear. It is to re-establish an idea of self-governing citizenship. This automatically begins to reverse the tide of yobbish behaviour steming from a small but growing minority of families who fail to nurture their children properly.

While there will be a need for a specially designed programme for this group, such a programme must be seen as part of an advance encompassing the entire population. This programme has to aim at nothing less than virtuous behaviour becoming once again an unquestioned norm.

How and where might such a political campaign begin? If the aim is to make the advance a general one, covering everyone, where such a campaign should open begins to answer itself. It is within schools. Success here will be pivotal to the outcome of the attempt to recast a sense of citizenship in Britain in the new millennium.

Sure Start programmes for young people from birth to fourteen have a pivotal part to play. The earlier one starts, the greater the chance of breaking the cycle of disadvantage. All Sure Start programmes should have a role in putting flesh on to the contract signed at the naming ceremony, and particularly offering help on how to be a good parent in safeguarding and nurturing children.

A second stage comes with the contracts to be developed as pupils move to primary schools. Contracts between schools and parents are now par for the course. Nursery and reception classes do much to counter the disadvantage all too many children still face. The aim must be to build on the advice and support Sure Start programmes have already begun to deliver in this respect.

Secondary schools present a key opportunity to achieve two objectives. The first is to build a behavioural contract. The second is to begin to develop the skills of successful parenthood. Once again, a note of hopeful optimism can be sounded on both fronts.

Schools are beginning to negotiate the basis of what could become school/home contracts. And from what the punters say, it is clear that the idea of parenting classes is not going to be forced on to a reluctant, let alone a sullen populace. What might a school contract look like? And what shape should the parenting classes take?

School contracts

Schools are already introducing contracts. But my experience of visiting schools is that a standard contract is simply issued at the entry of a pupil to a secondary school, parents are required to sign it and that, more or less, is that. The manner in which these contracts are issued suggests that many schools see them as yet another task imposed upon them by government edict.

Such school contracts need to move on and embrace a radically different role. The task must be to open up negotiations between all three parties, parents, pupils and schools, so that what emerges is more recognisably a contract which tries to live up to its name. The advantage of so doing is fairly obvious.

Parents and pupils become stakeholders to the enterprise. The content of the contracts would be much improved and might thereby begin to take on a life of their own. Moreover, the signing of the contract would be an important public event that will offer another opportunity of gaining support for an enforceable contract.

Pupils I have spoken to have clear views on what the contract should be about. They also are quite insistent on how the contract should be viewed. Standard contracts lay down how pupils should behave to each other, countering bullying rightly features prominently. This emphasis is shared by pupils, but they go further.

When asked by what principles their behaviour to others should be judged, and how other people, including teachers, should behave to them, there comes a single answer. Pupils unanimously believe that they should behave to others as they wish others to behave to themselves. The national survey which pinpointed a move to good citizenship being largely viewed in terms of respect for others is borne out in the classroom.

This very personal judgement about proper behaviour does not lead in any way to an impossibly loose guide to behaviour. When asked what then is unacceptable behaviour all the answers mention those actions that strike at, let alone undermine, the dignity of another person. Each of the pupils in replying to my question had a clear idea of what they understood by human dignity. If the answers I have gained from Birkenhead pupils are reflective of other pupils throughout the country, the task of re-establishing a right view of citizenship is clearly less daunting than it would otherwise be. The central value which has to lie at the heart of a sustainable citizenship is alive and well.

The moral capital we have inherited has deposited the clearest of ideas on how each of us should conduct our behaviour with other people. *Neighbours from Hell* sees the initiation of contracts over most areas of public life as the best means of strengthening this view about behaviour and citizenship in Britain today.

Respect in practice

Pupils also stress that their discussions in class on contracts, citizenship and similar issues, should be bound by rules of behaviour which again try to ensure that a person's dignity is protected. The pupils insisted that discussions in the classroom were sacrosanct and that no one should be laughed at afterwards because of the views they had put forward in debate. This objective is one which in all probability is not always met, but its aim is noble.

Pupils also had a clear idea on the policing of contracts. A contract openly negotiated would be policed in part by peer group pressure. But such a contract also raises the intriguing possibility of an authority for other sanctions. Pupils believe that persistent breaking of the contract should lead to suspensions from school. Openly negotiated contracts would therefore offer a new authority for school exclusions.

What additions would pupils make to their standard contract? Again the answer I gained was near universal. They wanted to keep part of the contract to centre on a school's duty to do all in its power to help them succeed in their examinations.

Most of the participators to our discussion knew only too well that exam successes were the best gateway into work. For a contract which does not match their behaviour and effort with a duty on the school in this respect is at once devalued.

No sensible contract can guarantee such success, of course, but the demand itself gives an opportunity to spell out the conditions which make success more likely. It returns the conversation to behaviour, and effort by pupils and teachers alike, and makes the different parts of the contract reinforcing.

One way of reviewing the school's success in its teaching programme would be for this aspect of the contract, and other aspects too, to be reviewed regularly through the school's council. The process of election to this body, and its powers would also feature in the contract, and would offer a crucial teaching agent on how democratic bodies work. In one junior school council in Birkenhead, I was impressed by how council representatives were learning what to do when they had failed to carry a majority of their fellow council members with them, and how they reported back failure as well as success to the class who had elected them.

Building up the contract

Having open school contracts that are genuine agreements between the three parties, parent, pupils and teachers, will throw up, no doubt, some surprising suggestions on what schools might offer pupils and parents. They would also offer an important opportunity for the teaching staff to shape the contract. There are contracts to be struck as children go into junior school and one which will be extended as pupils move into secondary education.

Once the contracts are agreed between the different parties they will offer another important opportunity to make a public ceremony speak of the wider aims of citizenship to which society is committed. Schools should schedule times at the start of the school year, at different times and on different days, including the weekend, when parents could come into school to discuss in groups what they wish to see as part of the contract. Pupils would undertake a similar exercise in class. The draft contract, based first on a standard format issued by the government, and then the one based on the previous year's deliberations, would be revised, agreed and then signed.

The signing ceremony should be scheduled as important days in the life of the school. The heart of the contract would be the kind of citizen the country wishes to see come from each pupil. What makes an ideal citizen would be promoted throughout the life of the school. Behaviour in class, in and around school, would be modelled on it. School societies would enhance this ideal in the way such organisations are run and work.

The prestigious positions for pupils within the school would be linked to the exercise of these key values on character, personality and conduct. The display of these attributes would be rewarded by advancement to prestigious positions for pupils within the school community. Prefects, class representatives and sports leadership awards, for example, would be linked to these citizenship values.

Successful parents

Pupils were again pretty unanimous that one of the topics they should seriously study at school should be parenting. The strength of feeling on this topic surprised me on a number of counts.

There were no noticeable differences in the response to questions about parenting classes amongst the older pupils with whom I held discussions, whether they were male or female. Nor was there any different between, what I might call, the rugby team members of the class and the others. If anything, the former group were the most confident in emphasising their wish for such a course.

One other aspect of these discussions leads to surprise. Many, perhaps most of the pupils, live with only one parent, and for some that one parent had such big problems with drugs or drink that these pupils were, to all intents and purposes, on their own.

Yet there was no embarrassment at my raising the issue of parenting classes. Nor was there any way in which I could tell from the discussion which pupils might have happy homes and those for whom this was still an ideal. Indeed, the wish to build a happy family was so resolutely expressed that this aspect of my discussions knocked me sideways.

Newly acquired parenthood

The schools' programme on parenting should develop two themes, and the link between these twin themes will be part of the course. The implementation of a school/home contract will centre on behaviour: how individual pupils behave to other pupils and to the school staff and, in return, the reciprocal basis of this contract.

The re-emphasise on social virtues – how to regard other people – needs to form the key plank of a parenting course. Because of the time parents should spend with their children they naturally become their offspring's chief role models. The more successful then the citizenship course is, the more successful future parents will be in one of their main investments bestowed on their children.

The parenting courses, in addition, should cover two other major themes. A better understanding of what the major needs of all children are should be central to the course. Likewise, the building up of a checklist of how best to promote healthy and happy children should form the other. What are the most profitable acts potential parents can perform to give the best start in life to each of their children?

An important part of this course should be the study of what is expected of parents who adopt so that this becomes a framework for all parents [see panel on page 121]. The careful preparation for success here is in stark contrast to the total absence of help and training for one of the most important acts parents undertake. The classes, which will go through the stages of becoming parents by adoption, will allow much role playing of what is required for forming a natural family.

The preferences of pupils to be good parents, and the wish to be helped to achieve this objective, are shared by parents themselves. There is a clear demand from this group to learn much more about these skills.

A survey of parents' needs, carried out by Exploring Parenthood through Sainsbury's magazine, reported over 60 per cent of the 14,000 parents who responded registered a wish for parenting skills training. Most of these parents recorded that such courses were not on offer. A very few courses, many no doubt of quite outstanding value, are run on a local basis, and the material from some of these courses is made more widely available.

The supply of these courses in no way matches their geographical demand. Where courses are run, education psychologists and health visitors are most heavily involved. This involvement by those specialists is approved by parents and is again a pointer to the kind of people and skills to which parents most wish to have access.

There is also a clear recognition amongst many parents that sometimes they need to seek outside help, and such recognition is translated into action. Here is yet another sign that advance on this front will be pushing, if not at an open door, one which is clearly ajar.

Every parent a wanted parent

The assumption is that individuals acquire by osmosis the ability to be good parents. Consider the weakness of this when individuals seek to become parents by adoption. To begin making such an application requires couples and individuals to pass through four qualifying barriers. Once this process is successfully completed, six other qualifying barriers have to be successfully mounted before parenthood can be assumed.

In the first place parents have to express a positive interest that they wish to adopt. It is a conscious decision. Every adopted child is by definition a wanted child. Once they have made an initial enquiry, the adoption agency may ask the couple to an information meeting where they will meet and talk with social workers and adoptive parents. Here couples will gain firsthand experience of adopting a child. If this interview meets with success, a social worker will then arrange to meet the couple so that they can find out more about what will happen if they decide to go ahead for adoption. Once that barrier has been surmounted, couples and individuals begin to fill in application forms and checks are made by the police and by the local authority on the adoptive parents' record and background.

Once these initial four steps have been taken, six further qualifying conditions have to be fulfilled by the would-be parents. A longer period of preparation begins, and during this time some very important thinking about making a lifetime's commitment to a child is debated with the potential parents. What are the needs of an adopted child, and can the potential parents make the sort of commitment that will really make a difference to a child's life, are some of the questions considered. Parents then undertake a full medical examination and provide the agency with two personal referees.

The next step is for a home study visit, where a social worker will work together with the potential parents to produce a home study report. How would an adoptive child fit into the home environment?

The material thereby gathered goes forward to an adoption panel which begins to consider whether or not the adopted parents are suitable candidates. Once parents are approved the adoption agency, as the next step, begins to consider whether there are children waiting for adoption locally who might be suitable. Once a child has been identified, the potential parents are given full information about their background and the parents are asked whether they wish to proceed. On the guidance issued by the Department of Health it is noticeable that at this stage potential parents are reminded that 'you are not on your own', a vivid contrast to how most natural parents feel once they have taken their baby home.

Once these nine steps have been negotiated successfully, and the adoptive child has settled down successfully in his or her new family, the adoptive parents may apply to the court for an adoption order to be made.

Outside help

There has been one major national survey measuring the extent to which, and the reasons why, parents sought advice and help with their children. The survey concluded however that its 'most striking' finding was how few parents reported having problems with their children.

There is clearly a debate to have over the definition of few. The results detail that one in five parents covered in this large survey reported they had sought advice from outside their family. As it is likely that some parents would be unwilling to recognise that they have problems with their children, while others might not wish to admit in a survey that that is the very position they find themselves in, a total of one in five parents reporting to an outsider, that, sometimes, their children become too much for them to manage by themselves successfully, is a very significant result indeed.

In four ways the survey results suggest how best to shape policy. First, health problems were the most reported reasons for seeking help by parents with children under five. If learning and behavioural difficulties are added together this group then jumps to the second most significant reason given by parents for facing difficulties. For older children, behaviour problems were the most common issue on which advice was sought.

Second, over four out of five parents chose a non-family member from whom to seek advice, although most of them reported that they had discussed the issue with their partners, where such a person existed. The persons most likely to be approached were a doctor or a teacher.

Third, more problems were reported by poorer parents, and non-working parents, than richer and working parents. In fact, poorer parents were twice as likely to seek advice than their working counterparts. The exception here was of single mothers at work who reported a higher incidence of problems than non-working families.

Fourth, behavioural and other problems at school were not clearly distinguished and probably many such problems were associated with the bullying of poorer children by their richer peers.

The acceptance of health visitors and medical staff as refuges where practical help can be gained hints clearly on who should be involved in building up and teaching the parenting classes in schools, as well as for those who are shortly to become parents.

Top grade

How should such courses be rated when taught within schools? As I will argue, they need to be part of a somewhat larger syllabus centring on citizenship. At the moment a citizenship course rates at only half a

GCSE. Consequently, few pupils wish to take it and it is not a subject which rates highly as one teachers wish to teach. It is not, generally speaking, a subject which helps promote a teacher's career.

If citizenship is to be valued as the most important group of attitudes and skills a school will help to give to pupils, three reforms suggest themselves. The subject has to rate at least equal to one GCSE, and I argue that to emphasise its strategic role, citizenship passes should count as two GCSEs.

The courses in citizenship have to be compulsory. Likewise, the status of teaching this subject has to be changed over and above it becoming a compulsory examination subject. Giving the course a double weighting in GCSE successes, and thereby potentially affecting the position of the school in the national league tables, would ensure that responsibility for these courses by teachers would become coveted, as success on this front would weigh disproportionately in the school's examination record.

Conclusion

For too long society has taken for granted that families would nurture those social virtues crucial for a civilised existence. Where the knowledge does not exist within families to hand on to their children, schools must fill the breach. As more and more families become dysfunctional in one of their major duties, it becomes ever more important for both the knowledge and values about parenthood and citizenship to become a cornerstone of a revamped curriculum. Not only must the national curriculum be remodelled, but the weighting of exam results and the rewards to teachers must reflect the importance and the urgency of this new agenda.

11. The politics of behaviour . . . again

Introduction

Countering anti-social behaviour is a major priority for voters. Building up a counter-strategy offers parliament an important opportunity to forge new links with an increasingly alienated electorate. The skills of high politics need to be matched with grass roots insights and enthusiasm. Countering effectively anti-social behaviour also offers an ideal opportunity to reform the way parliament and the executive works. Countering anti-social behaviour needs to be built into the cabinet committee structure as well as being reflected in the select committee system of the Commons.

Gird up your loins

A new public philosophy has to be crafted, agreed and enforced. The task is monumental but achievable. Much of the old beliefs on decent behaviour remain with the majority of the population.

Equally important, the coming generation has given its own take on this inheritance. The results of the survey of how younger people perceive citizenship augers well. Specific values are in at the expense of vague notions about how societies might or should work.

Human nature is also on our side. Most of us like to look up to those who excel in what are generally regarded as the good things in life. Many of us take role models from sportsmen and women, pop idols, great military leaders and even entrepreneurs.

At a more local level, the people who make the greatest mark on us are our parents and teachers. The natural urge of human beings to try and emulate the best in those they admire needs to be built upon as part of the building blocks for any citizenship. But while these are huge pluses to add into the equation, the weight of the minus side should not be underestimated. Anti-social behaviour is on the march. The measures the government has taken, although much welcomed as signs of its seriousness, will not contain the new nihilists, let alone strike down their recruiting sergeants. The government accepts this and has promised to continue to develop its counter-strategy.

The politics of behaviour has ushered in a new political era. Gone largely is the old class agenda. From who owns what we have moved swiftly to who does what, and in what manner. The political axis has shifted. Politicians need to adapt to the emerging agenda of voters. What kind of people we are, what our values are, and how we regard other people, is now the stuff of politics. Voters wish to see our characters as citizens move firmly onto the centre ground of politics.

Politics' role

Without clear, determined and talented leadership this enterprise, upon which the voters are anxious to embark, will flounder. As at any of the turning points in history, the role of political leadership can be crucial to the outcome of events.

The politics of behaviour requires resolution and vision. Success demands the Prime Minister and his entire government being signed up to the project as though the nation's future depended on their effort, as, in the longer-run, it assuredly does. And that commitment needs to be reflected in the cabinet committee structure. Rolling out an effective anti-social behaviour strategy requires pulling together an expertise which straddles most of the main departments of state.

The politics of behaviour has to become a main obsession of governing. Tackling the breakdown of a common decencies culture requires an effort equal to that which is mobilised for war, for war this is in one of the most difficult of terrains. In no way is this a plea for old fashioned elitist or, as is more ostentatiously dubbed, high politics. The top table is necessary, but those sitting around it need to earn their next meal. High politics has to reach out and meet the politics emerging from the grass roots.

Root causes

The government's latest publication on countering anti-social behaviour is full of insights and valuable suggestions on how best to counter the plague of disorder which now marks the lives of so many people. What it does not do is to seek out the causes of such behaviour, the like of which Britain has not seen for well over a century.

Neighbours from Hell sets out the root causes of the present unrest. Civilised behaviour as we know it is heavily dependent on the practice of three cardinal social virtues – politeness, considerateness and thoughtfulness.

Civility is born and nurtured in families. But the failure of families to practice these social virtues leads some individuals to continually disruptive and aggressive behaviour, which makes life for those living in the vicinity well nigh impossible.

Worst still, in the absence of a clear public philosophy which lays down what constitutes decent behaviour, we are witnessing a withdrawal of a considerably larger group of the population who now fail to rally to defend a common decency culture. The feelings and behaviour of this growing group of the population was described in chapter two. Reform has to address this group too.

It is here that the law has a crucial part to play. Law cannot make us moral individuals. What it can do is restrain the worst side of our nature. Moreover, by setting down clear guidelines on acceptable behaviour, it reinforces peer group pressure towards that objective.

Social Highway Code

Setting out what is expected of each of us in a series of citizenship contracts will focus clearly on what society will accept in terms of behaviour and what it will not. The contracts will, in effect, be establishing a social highway code. Such a code will strengthen the resolve of the fast disengaging middle group, which was also described in chapter two. The contracts will likewise lay down clear guidelines for behaviour for the socially disruptive elements.

The basic rules of behaviour, and basic duties, will be set out for us clearly and succinctly at each of the main points in our rites of passage – at birth, at school and at work. A declaration of success comes with retirement. The contracts will have two parts – duties which must be carried out by individuals, and duties society will carry out in turn to advance each individual's and family's wellbeing. The contracts will, in Burke's imagery, repair the riverbank within which society safely operates.

This social highway code will be of particular value to those parents who know they are not currently succeeding as well as they would like. Early intervention is crucial. Repairing the damage at a late stage when children are behaving badly is of course a harder task. The parents I have spoken to who have looked for help in parenting classes are depressed by their own failure and wish to do better.

Without self pity, they stress that parenting is a huge task and they were cast into this role with no help other than the model their parents gave them. Making parenting courses available for all parents throughout the country must be part of an effective strategy. They should run as part of ante-natal sessions. The best of existing courses need to be universalised quickly. Where parents have failed, it is in everybody's interest to help them succeed in building on the love they have for their children, and for those other aspects of parenting in which they excel.

Where a natural discipline of parent to child has failed, surrogate parents are required to check quickly and effectively unacceptable behaviour. This is a task that should be allocated to the police. The levying of a set number of penalty points against bad behaviour, as described in chapter eight, should lead to an immediate imposition of an anti-social behaviour order. Seeing disorder checked is likely to counter disorder spreading. The surrogate parents, as well as checking bad behaviour, should have the power to ensure that the offender undertakes a task beneficial to the community. After, that is, they have met face to face with those individuals who have been on the receiving end of their unacceptable behaviour.

Police Resources

There is no way the police will be able to carry out their new tasks described here, let alone ensure a more effective enforcement of existing legislation against lawlessness, without a significant increase in their budget. This is not a plea for showering them with resources a la NHS model. As the NHS illustrates, it is difficult for an organisation to spend well a very rapid and substantial increase in its budget.

A significant increase in the police budget over the longer-term is required, however. Yet we live in an age when taxpayers will use their vote to strike against political parties who take yet more money from their hard won earnings. Unless, that is, the new revenue is tied to specific spending programmes and the results of the new money can be seen fairly quickly and clearly. I sense there is a willingness by the electorate to increase the police budget, over time, by a very significant amount. But taxpayers want to see their increased tax spent in a way in which they approve. Local authorities should be given the power to hold a referendum on designated increases in council tax being covenanted to the police budget. Those areas that vote in favour of allocating more money would see more police in their area. No taxation without clearly discernable delivery will become the new cry.

Welfare contracts

The social highway code should be spelt out in a whole series of welfare contracts. Because this will be seen as a fundamental change in how society operates, the reasons for linking good behaviour and best practice to drawing benefit needs to be explained fully and on as many opportunities as possible.

Why are such welfare contracts needed? There are three reasons why benefits should be used to help entrench universal contracts.

The first is that the exceptional period into which we are fast moving, with a growing collapse in decent behaviour, requires new boundaries to be drawn that can be successfully manned. Benefits provide such a boundary as, between them, they provide a universal coverage for those people most likely to commit anti-social behavioural acts.

A second reason why benefit sanctions should become a key part of enforcing an effective anti-social behaviour strategy is that benefits are increasingly seen as a mark of the rights of citizenship. Indeed, opposition to such a proposal is most likely to come from that quarter arguing most strongly the citizenship aspect of welfare. But citizenship cannot be a one-way ticket. Full citizenship imposes duties as well as bestowing rights.

The third reason for enrolling benefit entitlement into a much wider strategy against anti-social behaviour is that they offer the easiest way to impose fines. Imposing fines is not the aim of strategies to counter anti-social behaviour. But at the end of the line, those behaving in an unacceptable manner must be sanctioned.

Paying fines in most areas of the country is now almost a voluntary activity. Imposing penalties at source, for that is what deductions in benefit will entail, offers a more effective way of penalising those people who fail to live up to the minimum requirements of citizenship.

Education as parents

The strategy lying behind *Neighbours from Hell* will fail if the new politics is simply confined to trying to curb unacceptable behaviour. Such sanctions are clearly necessary. The line against the new nihilists has to be held. But the cultivation of the cardinal social virtues which will underpin an agreed social philosophy requires even greater attention.

Here schools have a pivotal role. Where else are people to gain what, in terms of the past, they gain from being brought up in a successful family if it is not in school? What is the point of seeing schools as a passport to success at work – which is, of course, of crucial importance – if, at the same time, some of the school graduates are active recruits to the new barbarism?

Placing the task on schools of preparing their charges to be full and effective citizens means a reweighting of what schools should do. New mandatory tasks must be matched with cuts to their existing work programme.

Demoting or abolishing part of the syllabus, so that citizenship and parenthood is made a major core of the national curriculum, is not primarily an issue of money. But reformers need to be careful before they place yet more tasks on schools. All too many of these schools have been hyper-active over the past decade in turning failing establishments into clear successes.

Remapping the syllabus will be a major task, even though it will be building on some work already set in hand. A major initiative is, however, needed. When it was agreed that the way science was taught in schools needed to be rethought root and branch, the Nuffield Foundation, in the form of the Nuffield Science Project, planned a curriculum revolution. The work of that Foundation on science teaching now needs to be matched in the teaching of citizenship and parenthood. There are two organisations focusing on the teaching of citizenship, which should become the backbone of a national initiative. They are the Citizenship Foundation and the National Centre for Citizenship and the Law.

Keeping on course

The political pressure needs to be maintained in effectively countering anti-social behaviour. It is necessary for the government to give a clear unambiguous commitment to finding ways of beating such behaviour. It is clear that there is no panacea which, if enacted, would revert us back to a peaceable kingdom. Strategies have to be thought out, announced, implemented and then amended as society painfully builds up its knowledge on what works, and what doesn't work, in this new area of politics.

While governments have their role, parliament has a key role to play as well. Governments are easily buffeted by what Harold Macmillan once termed as 'events'. Northern Ireland, Iraq, the Middle East, and the growing famine in Africa are a few examples of issues which can quickly blow up and consume a great deal of the government's time.

While parliament obviously reacts to these events, it has its own role in helping shape events. Each Member of the House of Commons represents a constituency and constituencies provide MPs with the most valuable of tutorials. They teach MPs how the political agenda is changing. At one time the function of the House of Commons was to make and unmake governments. That is a task which now generally falls to the electorate when it casts its votes during a general election. The resulting political vacuum is being filled as parliament takes on what were once described by the constitutional observer, Walter Bagehot, as the functions of the monarch. Parliament has the right to be consulted, to advise and to warn.

Parliament's institutions are developing in response to fulfilling its role in giving advice to government. One of the most important parliamentary reforms during the 1979 Parliament was to establish a series of select commitees shadowing each government department. The role of select commitees, which spanned a number of departments, largely fell into abeyance.

Countering anti-social behaviour is not the province of a single government department. It is therefore necessary, if Parliament is to carry out its advising functions effectively, that select commitees are established which take as their theme topics that span across departments. Anti-social behaviour is one such issue.

Whereas events all too often buffet governments on a day to day basis select commitees are anchored by their subject matter. Moreover, a select commitee working well will not merely respond to a government's programme, important as this is, but will map out a new agenda so that the select commitee itself begins to set the political agenda. A select commitee on anti-social behaviour could carry out such a role. The material in this book has taken six months to collect and write. A select commitee would ensure that a group of MPs were commissioned to keep the programme on course. The committee would map out a programme, commission work, invite witnesses and plan meetings around the country in order to ascertain how people were being affected by anti-social behaviour, and would determine the best ideas for countering this, which might then be applied on a wider basis.

They would seek to ensure their events were covered by the media. There would then be an inevitable feedback from some voters while many more of the electorate would see parliament take up issues of major concern to themselves and their families. Democracy would be strengthened. A select commitee is not a panacea but it could play an important part in ensuring that a committed group of MPs make sure countering anti-social behaviour remains high up on the political agenda for action.

Conclusions

Holding the line

1. The first task is to protect more effectively the victims of anti-social behaviour. The police and community police should be given the powers of surrogate parents. A penalty points system is proposed. Three warnings from surrogate parents will lead to an automatic anti-social behaviour order being imposed on the offender. The order, time limited, will remain in force unless overturned by the courts. The surrogate parents, as well as having the power to restrict behaviour, will also have the power to request specific actions of good behaviour to the local community. These quick fix orders will run alongside traditional anti-social behaviour orders.

2. The police must be more actively involved in fighting as opposed to recording crime and anti-social behaviour. They do not have the resources to do so effectively. We need to move swiftly to an expectation that every crime is an act which will be followed up seriously by the police with the aim of bringing the perpetrators to justice. Because the police are so understaffed, crime and anti-social behaviour cannot be taken with the utmost seriousness. A fifty per cent increase in the police budget is required. Getting the right people to fill these new posts will take time. A new tax contract will be required to raise the necessary funds to finance such an increase. Local referenda will decide if voters wish to pay more so that there will be more police on their streets.

Readjusting the balance

3. Anti-social behaviour falls most severely on ordinary families and the poor. While many other people experience acts of anti-social

behaviour, for example, as they travel around, it is poorer people who are most likely to be bugged on a regular basis. The plague-like impact of anti-social behaviour is not reflected in the resources put to counter and prosecute offenders: existing police manpower is not spread to reflect accurately the pattern of crime and anti-social behaviour. It needs to be. In addition, electing to pay more for police, which operate only in the areas which pay for them, will allow a major increase in the number of police. But consumer sovereignty needs to be taken further. The Crown Prosecution Service should have an office and staff in each constituency, and its chief officer should be elected and accountable to that area for the CPS's prosecution policy. By making these important legal posts electable, crimes that ordinary people think are most important will be reflected in the clear-up and prosecution rates of that area. As electing these posts on a four year basis will give local people an effective say in countering crime, I would be surprised if the turnout at these elections was not as high as at the general election.

4. Weighting our legal system so that it is more in favour of the innocent needs also to be part of the agenda. The reforms here must range from ensuring that witnesses at court have separate waiting rooms, so that the bullying which is usually part of anti-social behaviour, and of other crimes too, does not continue right up to the court appearance, to a rebalancing of how the European Convention on Human Rights is interpreted. The Convention, pursuing a most important ideal, operates all too often counter to most people's sense of fairness. The common good must be given an appropriate weighting when the rights of individuals or minorities are considered. The ruling that taking housing benefit away from neighbours from hell is likely to denigrate the culprits would

be laughable if rulings such as this were not part of the human rights agenda as we experience it in this country.

A self-governing democracy

5. The aim of a holding the line strategy is precisely that; of drawing clearer boundaries dividing acceptable from unacceptable behaviour. The main emphasis of *Neighbours from Hell* is to re-enforce and re-teach the common decencies which centre on a proper consideration of other people's needs. Sanctions will have to play some part in this strategy, though the aim is not to apply sanctions for sanctions sake. Macho politics are replaced by a more subtle approach where sanctions are used so appropriately that political offenders know they cannot call the system's bluff. Hence the plea for an expansion of secure units for young people sentenced by the court. The announcement of such a building programme will, if used properly, help to create a climate where young offenders see the white of society's eyes.

6. While holding the line in present circumstances is all important, societies function best when its citizens are self-governing. Hence the contract framework which *Neighbours from Hell* advocates. Each part of this contract reinforces a set of common decencies and thereby teaches at regular intervals each new generation what is expected of them.

7. Individuals function best if they know in advance the rules of the game. Through the main events of each of our lives, from birth, through schools, claiming benefit, and at retirement, society should use each milestone as a means of teaching once again what duties each of us have to fulfil before we can tap into the array of rights society also guarantees us.

8. Crucial to the whole process is the role of parents. The better parents perform, the more happy and contented society is. Just as wars are too important to be left to the generals, so parenting is too vital to society's wellbeing to be left to parents unaided. Some people are naturally good parents. Others do not gain the necessary skills by osmosis. Love cannot be bought but nurturing can be taught. Imparting the skills of good parenthood should become a major part of the national curriculum, and while other subjects will be taught through it, for example, the use of good English, other disciplines, such as biological sciences, will also become a central part of the curriculum.

9. The importance of anti-social behaviour to voters must be reflected in the cabinet committee structure and in the way the House of Commons works. A set group of Ministers, on the one hand, and MPs on the other, should be charged with developing a strategy to counter anti-social behaviour, which is now one of the big issues for voters. It is not just a matter of joined up government, but of joining government up with the electorate.

10 A programme to counter anti-social behaviour has to be multi-faceted. It must consist of measures to hold the line against the new barbarianism more and more of us are experiencing in our every day lives. It must also consider the recruiting sergeants to the new nihilist forces in our midst, and begin dealing simultaneously with these. The social virtues so necessary to civilised living are born and nurtured in families. Any effective counter-strategy must therefore seek ways of spreading the success of many families in this respect to a small but growing minority who fail to nurture their children well. What the new civility amounts to has to be enshrined in a new contract culture, and here welfare must play a vital role. And where families fail, only schools can step into the void.

Sources

The book which makes the case for a step change in politics, from an exclusive concern about the operation of markets to centring on the character of the citizenry, is George F. Will, *Statescraft as Soulcraft*, Simon and Schuster, 1983. A similarly important work on the culture of politics, and its transition from a class agenda, is Lawrence M. Mead's *The New Politics of Poverty*, Basic Books, 1981.

Information on what is currently known about the extent of anti-social behaviour comes from a number of sources. The DETR *Analysis of the Survey of English Housing 1997-1998* as well as the Audit Commission's, *Safety in Numbers,* 1999 are important sources. This latter report details how anti-social behaviour contributes to high levels of fear of crime and how many of the poor themselves are affected by anti-social behaviour. So too does J. Nixon, C. Hunter and S. Shayer, *The Use of Legal Remedies by Social Landlords to Deal with Neighbour Nuisance*, Centre for Regional Economic and Social Research, Sheffield Hallam University, 1999 and NACRO's *Nuisance and Anti-Social Behaviour – a report of a survey of local authority housing departments*, 1998.

Some idea of the cost of anti-social behaviour is to be found in *The Management of Neighbourhood Complaints in Social Housing*, which Aldbourne Associates published in 1993. A model of its kind is S. Campbell's *Review of Anti-Social Behaviour Orders,* Home Office Research Study 236, 2002.

Data on the increase in anti-social behaviour is to be found in the Audit Commission's *Safety in Numbers*, 1999. J Wilson and G Kelling, 'Broken Windows', *Atlantic Monthly*, 1992 gives the information on how quickly neighbourhoods can decline if anti-social behaviour is left unchecked. This article lays the basis for a more constructive debate on how best to use police resources. How serious such disputes can become comes from *Neighbour Disputes*, a study by J. Dignan, A. Sorsby, and J. Hibbert, which the University of Sheffield published in 1996.

The survey on attitudes as to what makes good citizens can be found in *The Big Turn Off: attitudes of young people to government, citizenship and community*, by Madsen Pirie and Robert M. Worcester, Adam Smith, 2000. Ceridwen Roberts, Natalie Cronin, Tricia Dodd and Maureen Kelly are the authors of *A national study of parents and parenting problems*, Family Policy Studies Centre, 1995.

The Joseph Rowntree Foundation commissioned Clem Henricson to consider whether there is a case for a parents' code. His report appeared as *Government and Parenting*, which the Foundation published in 2003.

There are a number of major government initiatives on anti-social behaviour. A summary of these, together with a new agenda, can be found in *Respect and Responsibility – Taking a Stand Against Anti-Social Behaviour,* which the Home Office published (Cm 5778) in 2003.